1978

A WALK IN OTHER WORLDS
WITH DANTE

Benvenuti, Assisi.

Dante representing the 3rd. order of the Franciscans.

Attributed to Giotto.

Frontispiece

A
WALK IN OTHER WORLDS
WITH DANTE

BY

MARION S. BAINBRIGGE

WITH EIGHT FULL-PAGE PLATES

KENNIKAT PRESS
Port Washington, N. Y./London

A WALK IN OTHER WORLDS WITH DANTE

First published in 1914
Reissued in 1969 by Kennikat Press
Library of Congress Catalog Card No: 73-101024
SBN 8046-0691-9

Manufactured by Taylor Publishing Company   Dallas, Texas

AI BEGLI OCCHI

CHE LUCEVAN SEMPRE

DAL

PARADISO

PREFACE

' L'Alba vinceva l'ora mattutina
        Che fuggia innanzi, sì che di lontano
        Conobbi il tremolar della marina.'
                    Pur. i, 115.

HE dawn was conquering the morning hour which fled before it, so that from afar I recognised the trembling of the sea.'
These lines, written centuries ago by the Divine Poet, as perchance he gazed across the far-off Italian sea, came to my mind when I too stood watching the morning mists calmly sweeping up off the face of the winter's sea on the southern shores of England. They accurately described the glorious effect stretched out before me in words so far above one's own halting tongue that since then, in various circumstances of life, I have turned me to the leaves of the great Florentine with a marvel of bewilderment, that he, who lived so differently, should

yet have had such knowledge of the thoughts
and wants of human souls as to leave behind him
treasures of guiding, strengthening and elevating
ideas, clothed in language at once poetic, beautiful, and suitable for all time.

It is not given to all to have leisure or inclina-
tion either to penetrate deeply enough into the
long mazes of the *Divina Commedia*, or to study
the Italian language sufficiently to appreciate the
subtle touches and apt allusions which, when
pointed out, are such a help and delight. Therefore the most noticeable of these, with explanations, have been collected and arranged in this
little book, so that they may be readily found
and assimilated with very small effort by those
who have only a few moments to spare in this
hurrying age. Just as a gardener delves and
brings in vegetables to be prepared for his
master's table, so may a disciple dig for and
arrange in a handy basket the rich food which
is without doubt presented in this poem, much
overlaid as it certainly is by historical and metaphysical matter not to be grasped by the many.

This is not a commentary nor is the book

compiled from an argumentative or historical point of view: it is merely an endeavour to gather together in a compact form some of the beautiful and elevating thoughts which ought to be the possession not only of Italians, but of all those souls who are struggling in this Purgatory of Life. Together with Dante's own words quotations are added from commentaries on Dantesque literature, which has been so largely enriched by the grand perception and laborious study of the finest minds since that day when the Poet passed to the more perfect Light of Life at Ravenna in the year of our Lord 1321.

A list of books which may be consulted is annexed.

To keep the matter well in hand allusions to the different readings of the text have been avoided.

This book is a reply to many requests for simple information from those who say '*Dante is too deep*' for them. They seem unable to find exactly what they want, notwithstanding the large number of books already written upon the subject. It is hoped that this one may be a source of pleasure and help to them and to others who from various causes are unable to study profoundly the works of the Poet to whom reference is constantly made in the present day.

I acknowledge with gratitude the kind permission granted to use quotations by The Rt. Hon. Lord Tennyson, P.C., G.C.M.G., Horatio F. Brown, Esq. (Literary Executor to the late Mr. J. Addington Symonds), The Rev. Father Sebastian Bowden, The Oxford University Press, Messrs. Macmillan, Messrs. A. & C. Black, Messrs. Burns & Oates, Messrs. Kegan Paul, Trench, Trübner & Co. For the lines of Signor D'Annunzio thanks are due to the Editor of the *Corriere della Sera*, and to a learned Dantist for important assistance.

My hearty thanks for valuable counsel and encouragement are also offered to Mrs. G. C. Frederick, the Countess Martinengo Cesaresco, Miss Gertrude Leigh, and L. G. B., as well as to Edith M. Bainbrigge for much help in correcting, and also for her diagram of the White Rose of the Saints.

M. S. B.

London, 1914.

CONTENTS

PART III

DEL PURGATORIO

PART IV

DEL PARADISO

LIST OF ILLUSTRATIONS

xiii

In the performance of plain duty
Man mounts to his highest bliss.

Song Celestial. EDWIN ARNOLD.

I turn for consolation to the leaves
Of the great master of our Tuscan tongue
Whose words, like colored garnet-shirls in lava
Betray the heat in which they were engendered.

. . . .

In his song
I hear reverberate the gates of Florence
Closing upon him, never more to open,
But mingled with the sounds are melodies
Celestial from the gates of Paradise.
He came and he is gone. The people knew not
What manner of man was passing by their doors
Until he passed no more.

LONGFELLOW.

Leggere Dante è un dovere,
Rileggere è bisogno,
Sentirlo è presagio di grandezza.

NICCOLO TOMMASÉO.

To read Dante is a duty,
To re-read is a necessity,
To understand is a foretaste of Heaven.

TO DANTE

(WRITTEN AT REQUEST OF THE FLORENTINES)
1865

By ALFRED LORD TENNYSON

King, that hast reign'd six hundred years, and grown
In power, and ever growest, since thine own
Fair Florence honouring thy nativity,
Thy Florence now the crown of Italy,
Hath sought the tribute of a verse from me,
I, wearing but the garland of a day,
Cast at thy feet one flower that fades away.

Dante in the midway of his life.
Giotto.

[*To face p.* xvi.

PART I

INTRODUCTION

A

A Walk in other Worlds with Dante

INTRODUCTION

HE great poet of the middle ages who wrote the sacred poem to which 'all heaven and earth set their hand,' and which made the author 'grow lean' through the long years of exile, was Dante Alighieri. He was born in Florence, A.D. 1265, in the month of May. His father, Alighiero dei Alighieri, belonged to a family not noble but of very ancient descent and well connected. They counted among their ancestors the Knight Cacciaguida who fought in the Crusades under the Emperor Conrad III, and they lived in the quarter of Florence near to the Porta San Piero, where the remains of the house of Dante stood

until 1877, to be 'renovated' since then out of existence.

Their kinsmen and other good families dwelt near, and it was while visiting a neighbour with his father as a boy that he met and immediately worshipped the Beatrice of the *Divina Commedia*, who is generally identified with the youthful daughter of Folco Portinari. He wrote sonnets in her honour, esteemed himself most happy did he but see her pass along the streets, and wove such a veil of mystical imagination around her that there are those who maintain his 'Lady' to have been merely an abstraction. Much rather would we believe in the inspiration which Dante obtained from the contemplation of this his ideal woman, more glorified still when she 'passed into high Heaven' in 1290. Dante as became the son of a notary was very well educated, and he began in early youth to take an intelligent interest in the affairs of his country. He fought with the foremost cavalry in the battle of Campaldino at the age of twenty-four, and he gave in one of his epistles an account of this victory gained by the Florentine Guelphs over the Aretines, who were assisted by the outlawed Ghibellines. He was also present at the siege of Caprona.

Italy was in a very disturbed state during the middle ages, there was no sovereign ruler, no cohesion between either states or cities, each lived for itself alone, the chief aim of each being to get the better of the other on all occasions. The smallest incident served as a match to set ablaze the smouldering flames of discord. The quarrels inside the cities between the excitable warrior nobles entrenched in their towered palaces, and the turbulent burghers, were vastly aggravated by the machinations of the great parties of Guelphs and Ghibellines. Wars and tumults constantly broke out; these ended usually in the banishment of the weaker party, who, taking refuge in some other town, thought nothing of joining the enemies of their own city in fighting against her, could they by this means compass a return to their homes.

The origin of these names of Guelph and Ghibelline seems lost in oblivion, but one plausible theory assigns it to the outcome of a quarrel

between Guelph, or Guelfone Duke of Bavaria
and his enemy the Emperor Conrad II (1024–
1039), called il Ghibellino from the castle of
Geiblingen or Wäiblingen where he was born.
However this may be it seems certain that these
factions originating in Germany found their way
over the Alps, bringing discord and misery in
their train, somewhere about A.D. 1154 when the
Emperor Frederick Barbarossa made his descent
into Italy.   Pope Innocent III established three
Guelphic leagues in the year 1199, one on the
Adriatic shore, another in the valley of the Tiber,
and the third in Tuscany.

Practically these two great parties were composed on the one side of those who favoured
the Emperor, and on the other of those who
favoured the power of the Pope.

The Ghibellines were generally aristocratic and
despotic, but they encouraged freedom of thought
in order to promote revolt against the Church.

The Guelphs were loyal to the Pope and the
Church, but both parties were most rebellious
and undisciplined.

Florence, always more or less of a Guelph

stronghold, turned the Ghibellines out of the city in 1258, but the Florentine Guelphs sustained a severe defeat in 1260 at the battle of Montaperto at the hands of the Ghibellines of Siena, and the City of Flowers would then have been razed to the ground but for the splendid determination of Farinata dei Uberti, himself a Ghibelline. The Guelphs however returned to power in 1266, and carried all before them during the closing years of the thirteenth century.

The family of the Alighieri belonged to the Guelph party; the 'Ghibellinism' of Dante was probably of gradual growth. His dream for Italy was one of union and freedom as the centre of the Roman Empire, under the universal monarch who, as earthly representative and incarnation of justice, should make Roman law operative throughout the land. The possession of temporal power by the Pope was contrary to his judgment, as he considered that Pontiff to be the spiritual head of the Church only; and although to his life's end he remained a devout member of the Catholic Church into which he had been baptized, he very strongly deprecated the arrogant

pretensions and wide schemes of worldly aggrandisement adopted by those who called themselves
God's Vicegerents, but whose quarrels with
Emperors and Kings made for anything but
peace upon earth.

After Dante's banishment from Florence he
and other exiled White Guelphs allied themselves
with the outlawed Ghibellines, all alike anxious
to re-enter their beloved city; thus his name has
come down to posterity as the 'Great Ghibelline,' but as Mazzini said, 'he was really neither
Guelph nor Ghibelline ; he was *Italian.*'

Returning from the politics of the time to
Dante's personal history, we find that after his
youthful military experience he went back with
much zest to his literary education, soon showing his immense abilities and the great range
of his mind. He studied philosophy as a disciple of Aristotle, and while making himself
conversant with abstruse science and law he
revelled in Virgil's works, and explored the wide
region of ancient poetry, myth, and legend, thus
laying up inexhaustible stores of knowledge to be
woven eventually into his marvellous poem.   He

was however no recluse, for he joined in the sports and amusements of his companions which were then in vogue, such as falconry, the writing of clever rhymes, &c., and being of this sociable disposition he became well known in Florence, and was highly thought of on account of his learning and for his upright judgment.

It was needful at this time for important citizens, whether nobles or burghers, to enroll themselves in one of the seven greater Guilds or Arti in order to be eligible to hold office, so Dante joined the 6th Arte, that of the Physicians and Apothecaries ; and he served on their council between 1296 and 1301.

The government of the Commonwealth of Florence was then vested in the hands of six Priors who were elected from the members of these Trade Guilds, under a Gonfaloniere, the official who carried the Gonfalone or Standard of Justice ; they served only for two months at a time.

In the year 1300 Dante was elected one of the Priors at the age of thirty-five, and to this elevation he attributes all his future misfortunes, as he mentioned in one of his own epistles.

What he was like then may be seen in the fresco by his friend Giotto on the wall of the Chapel in the Bargello, uncovered from the whitewash of centuries through the perseverance of Mr. Kirkup, an Englishman, in 1840. It remains to show us the great poet wearing his distinctive cap and gown, a book under his arm, carrying a pomegranate in his right hand, walking in a Florentine procession with noble carriage and fine youthful face unscarred by the lines of sorrow which were afterwards marked upon it.

The cause of the ensuing troubles arose from the bitter feuds between two great families which rent in twain 'that lair of noxious beasts,' the city of Pistoia. This produced such contention that the heads of the parties were summoned to Florence in order that their grievances might be composed. Instead of peace the influx of these violent factions of the Neri and Bianchi resulted in the pestilence breaking out more desperately in Florence itself, because each party had friends and relations in the city, and sooner or later every man belonged either to the Neri who were in favour with the Pope, or to the

Bianchi who supported the constitutional government of the Priors. During Dante's Priorate
the quarrels raged so fiercely that by his advice,
which appears to have been most just and im-
partial, the heads of both parties were banished.
The Neri retired to Castello della Pieve in
Perugia, and the Bianchi to Sarzana.

In 1301 it is supposed that Dante went
as Ambassador to Rome on a pacific embassy
from the Commonwealth of Florence to Pope
Boniface VIII, but this unscrupulous and arrogant
Pontiff, while ostensibly treating with them, was
at the same time scheming with the banished
Neri faction for the introduction of Charles of
Valois into Florence.

Meantime the insalubrious climate of Sarzana
and the mortal illness of Guido Cavalcanti, one
of Dante's greatest friends, was made a pretext
for the return of the Bianchi to Florence. This
enraged the citizens, who most unjustly accused
Dante of being concerned with the return of this
faction, although having retired from the Priorate
he had nothing to do in the matter. With the
advent of Charles of Valois into Florence in 1301

the Neri party returned to power, vowing bitter
vengeance against the Bianchi who had opposed
the intrusion of this foreigner which was due to
the interference of the Pope.   Accordingly the
Neri proceeded to pronounce edicts of banishment upon about 600 of their fellow-citizens.
Among the most prominent was Dante himself,
and not only did they banish him in 1302 but his
property was confiscated, and fearing his powerful
personality the sentence of death was added later
should he fall into their hands.

Dante was not in Florence when these cruel
and desperate tidings reached him; he immediately repaired to Siena where he awaited
events, but no turn of the wheel of fortune
brought about a reversal of this terrible sentence.   When the case proved hopeless he
began that wandering life of exile spent in travel-
ling from place to place, now seeking refuge with
one patron now another, until at length about
the year 1316, or perhaps a little later, joined
by his sons Pietro and Jacopo and his daughter
Beatrice, he took up his abode as the honoured
guest and friend of Guido da Polenta at Ravenna.

Dante's wife Gemma dei Donati remained in Florence trying to recover some portion of his estate, and it is related that on one occasion when she was searching for title deeds in a chest, accompanied by a nephew, the latter found some papers which he sent to Dante. These may have been the first cantos of the *Inferno :* so, perhaps, but for the perspicacity of this young man, who seems to have resembled his uncle in face, the great poem might never have been completed.

A short notice of the Poet's contemporaries will help to bring him into perspective.

In England Henry III, Edward I, and Edward II succeeded each other on the throne, and in France Louis IX, Philip III, Philip IV, Louis X, and Philip V. The most noticeable of the many Popes who filled the Papal Chair were Celestine V, probably referred to as 'he who made the great refusal'; Boniface VIII, the poet's greatest enemy; and Clement V, who moved the Papal See to Avignon.

The massacre of the Sicilian Vespers took place

during Dante's lifetime, and Charles of Anjou, Charles II, and Robert were kings of Naples.

The Holy Roman Empire was governed by Rudolph, Adolphus, Albert I, and Henry of Luxemburg. The sudden death of the latter in 1313 at Buonconvento in Tuscany was a great blow to Dante, who looked upon him as the coming saviour of his country.

In art and letters Cimabue, Giotto, Franco of Bologna, S. Thomas Aquinas, S. Bonaventura, and Roger Bacon were at the height of their fame, while Petrarch and Boccaccio were only rising stars, being seventeen and eighteen years old respectively when the Poet died. Chaucer was not born till 1328, and printing was not invented for another century.

TABLE OF IMPORTANT EVENTS IN THE POET'S LIFE

Approximate
Dates

1265   Dante Alighieri was born on or about the 18th day of May 1265 A.D., in the city of Florence, and baptized in the baptistery of S. Giovanni.

When nine years old Dante met Beatrice Portinari.

Beatrice died.

Some years later Dante married Gemma dei Donati, by whom he had two sons, one daughter Beatrice, who became a nun at Ravenna, and a daughter Antonia mentioned in a document of the year 1332.

Pietro and Jacopo, his sons, were literary men; the former wrote a commentary on the *Divina Commedia*.

Dante entered the Arte of Physicians and Apothecaries, afterwards becoming one of the Priors of his native city.

He was possibly in Rome during the Jubilee held by Pope Boniface VIII, but his having gone as Ambassador is not proved, although he seems to have visited S. Gimignano on one occasion in that capacity.

A rising of the Neri faction in Florence drove the Bianchi out in 1302. Dante was exiled from Florence, and spent the rest of his life in various parts of Italy. According to some writers he went to Paris and Oxford, possibly to Arles and

Avignon, but it is certain that Siena, Verona, Lucca, the Casentino, Bologna, Arezzo, Pisa, and the Lunigiana were among his resting-places during his exile until he took up his abode at Ravenna.   In the pine woods there the *Paradiso* was completed.

1321   Dante died at Ravenna in 1321 from a fever caught on one of his visits to Venice, and Ravenna guards his honoured remains.

His chief works are the *Canzoni* and *Eclogues*, *La Vita Nuova*, *De Vulgari Eloquio*, *Il Convito*, *De Monarchia*, and *La Divina Commedia;* it is with the last that I have most to do.

Putting aside for the moment all the many and various readings of its much-disputed text, and the four different ways in which Dante himself allows that his great poem may be interpreted, we come at once to the question : *What may those who are not deep scholars learn from it?*   First, surely we shall find in Dante's Beatrice the most perfect and masterly portrait of an ideal woman, drawn with an unerring hand, filled in with exquisite delicate touches, alive with the warmth of love, beauty, and grace, and endowed with every virtue. A glorious conception! One of those calm, sympathetic women who recognise the responsibility of their power, and whose highest aim it is to raise men, and so to live that, instead of a rival, men may find in them the incentive to strive for noble aims.

Thus carrying out Tennyson's suggestive description of a woman, who was :

> Not perfect, nay, but full of tender wants,
> No Angel, but a dearer being, all dipt
> In Angel instincts, breathing Paradise,
> Interpreter between the Gods and men,
> Who looked all native to her place, and yet
> On tiptoe seem'd to touch upon a sphere
> Too gross to tread, and all male minds perforce
> Swayed to her from their orbits as they moved,
> And girdled her with music.
>
> *The Princess.*

It may be urged that Beatrice is the personification of Divine Wisdom and thus beyond our imitation or understanding ; but surely it behoves women to learn wisdom in order to enable them to ' help the wheels of this great world,' for those who know most will help best.

That women had high intellectual power was

B

well recognised in the Middle Ages, and in Italy it is known that many noble women were able administrators in managing estates, to say nothing of smaller households, while they were generally the patrons of art and occupied themselves in deep and learned studies.

Beatrice stands before us endowed with every intellectual gift; the fact that she has attained to perfect bliss and knowledge only makes her more solicitous to render help to her wandering worshipper lost in the maze of the 'selva selvaggia' (forest, savage, rough, and stern), which sadly describes the fate of many of us who are trying to climb the hill of life and to reach Terrestrial Paradise. Her loving thought is followed by prompt action. Without delay she acts on the suggestion of her willing helper, Lucia, and flies to entreat the aid of Virgil— that stately figure of calm discretion who stands in Limbo. He rescues Dante from his terrors and leads him through the Infernal Regions and Purgatory up to Terrestrial Paradise, where he finally leaves him in the keeping of his lady who shows him Paradise perfected.

Dean Church tells us that 'Dante's journey began under the Easter moon, on the eve of Good Friday; the days of mourning he spends in the regions of woe, and he issues forth to again behold the stars, to learn to die to sin and live to righteousness, very early in the morning as it began to dawn on the day of resurrection.' To draw Dante upward and onward until the final point is reached, and he attains to the vision of the Blessed Trinity, is the end and aim of the care of his adorable lady; she guides him with her eyes and her smile, and at the final moment she turns her gaze away from him and fixes it upon God.

Dante first saw her whom he calls 'il sol degli occhi miei' (the sun of my eyes) at the age of nine years, attired in a crimson robe, with a girdle round her waist—the beautiful Beatrice Portinari who became the adored object of his life, and of whom he says:

Dal primo giorno ch'io vidi 'l suo viso
  In questa vita, infino a questa vista
  Non m'è il seguire al mio cantar preciso.
                              Par. xxx, 28.

From the first day that I beheld her face
In this life, to the moment of this look,
The sequence of my song has ne'er been severed.
LONGFELLOW, transl.

She entered into his soul 'col fuoco ond io sempr' ardo' (with the fire with which I ever burn).   During her life he composed many sonnets about her, and when she died in 1290 his lament is beautiful and pathetic.   He closes the *Vita Nuova* with these remarkable words penned at the end of his last sonnet:

'After writing this sonnet there appeared to me a marvellous vision, in which I saw things which made me determine not to say anything further of this blessed one until I could more worthily speak of her.   In order to reach this end I study as much as I can, as she herself knoweth truly.   So that, if it shall please Him through whom everything lives that my life should last for some years, I hope to say of her that which has never yet been said of any woman.

'And then may it be pleasing to Him, who is the Lord of all courtesy, that my soul may go to see the glory of its lady, the blessed Beatrice, who gloriously gazes upon the face of Him who is blessed for evermore.   Laus Deo.'

The human personality of the Virgil of the *Divina Commedia* is never called in question, whilst a tempest of discussion swells around the name of Beatrice.   Was she a reality or was she merely a symbolical figure?

Since Folco Portinari, the father of a daughter called Beatrice who married Simone Bardi, is known to have been a wealthy Florentine citizen, living about 1275 in the same quarter of the city as the family of the Alighieri, it is reasonable to suppose that it was to his house Dante went on the occasion of the memorable meeting with his adored lady.   Folco Portinari's will is still extant, he gave large sums to charity, his memory is preserved on a monument in Florence where he founded a hospital which is still one of the best in the city.   Though Dante was himself of good family, he probably never thought of aspiring to the hand of Beatrice; he was perhaps too poor, she too rich, so he worshipped her from afar, and when she left this earth he wrote of her. While doing so ' La réalité se transfigure dans le symbole,' says Frédéric Ozanam, and perhaps there is truth in this view. The *Divina Commedia* is considered to be the apotheosis of Beatrice, but it may be more near the truth to call it the apotheosis of womankind, through the glorification, as in a parable, of the poet's ideal woman.

But certainly above and beyond this there is, secondly, the allegorical and mystical meaning, that exalting of Divine Wisdom which comes from above, the only sure and infallible guide for the souls of men wandering in this world seeking for light; Dante himself being the undoubted type of the soul of man.

Yes, Beatrice is imagined by him to have gone up into high heaven where the angels are at peace, and it is while sitting in the Empyrean, that calm, glorious place of rest, making one of the company of those who form the white Rose ' which with His blood Christ made His spouse,'

(La milizia santa
Che nel suo sangue Cristo fece sposa)

that she is roused by the piercing cry of Lucia,

the spirit of illumination, revealing to her the
perilous position of Dante. Warned by the
Blessed Virgin that the faithful one is in dire
need Lucia speeds to ask—

> . . . Beatrice, loda di Dio vera,
>   Chè non soccorri quei che t'amò tanto
>   Ch' uscio per te della volgare schiera?
> Non odi tu la pièta del suo pianto?
>   Non vedi tu la morte che il combatte
>   Su la fiumana, ove il mar non ha vanto?
>
> *Inf.* ii, 103.

> Beatrice, said she, the true praise of God,
>   Why succourest thou not him who loved thee so,
>   For thee he issued from the vulgar herd?
> Dost thou not hear the pity of his plaint?
>   Dost thou not see the death that combats him
>   Beside that flood, where ocean has no vaunt?
>
> LONGFELLOW, transl.

Promptly Beatrice flew then to where Virgil
walked in Limbo, with such haste as no one in
the world 'ever showed either for fortune, or to
escape punishment,' and with sweet persuasive
words implored the 'anima cortese mantovana'
(courteous Mantuan soul) to go to Dante's rescue.

Four reasons may be deduced for the choice of
Virgil as guide. Firstly, the immense admira-

tion for his writings which Dante entertained ; secondly, because in the 6th Book of the Æneid Virgil describes the journey of Æneas into the Infernal regions to visit his father Anchises ; thirdly, on account of his imperial ideas ; and fourthly, because Virgil was considered in the middle ages to be the greatest of allegorical writers.

The description of the interview of Beatrice with the great Latin poet is interesting.   Even in haste he has time to remark upon her eyes—

> Lucevan gli occhi suoi più che la Stella :
> E cominciommi a dir soave e piana
> Con angelica voce, in sua favella.
>
> *Inf.* ii, 55.

Her eyes shone brighter than the Star of Venus, and she began to say, gentle and low, with angelical voice in her own language . . . (namely, that soft voice which is so great a charm in women)—

"I am Beatrice, who begs you to go to the succour of my friend.

'Love moves me and makes me speak.'

Her beautiful eyes streaming with tears, she

yet waits to explain why she is not afraid to venture into that sad circle where Virgil dwells amongst those souls who never knew Christ. 'I do not fear to enter here, because one should only fear that which can do harm to others. Nothing else brings terror. I am so made by God, through His mercy, that your misery does not touch me and no flame of this fire can assail me.'—*Inf.* ii, 91.

This is very clearly meant to teach us that those who are kept by the power of God need not fear to lose the purity of their souls by going into any depths of trouble, or by coming in contact with evil doers in their efforts to rescue wanderers from their erring courses. They are kept from all harm, and the light in their own souls will burn the brighter for efforts to bring love and sympathy into the lives of others.

Persuaded by the urgency of Beatrice, Virgil takes Dante in charge, and he whose soul . . . 'quali i fioretti dal notturno gelo chinati e chiusi' (like flowerets touched by the night frost) had been overtaken by cowardice, raises his head and together they enter the gate of the Inferno

and commence the toilful journey. *Inf.* ii, 142.
Beatrice does not reveal herself to Dante until
Virgil can see no further, not until human wisdom
must give place to the divine.

Then, in the entrancing scene in Canto xxx
of the *Purgatorio*—

> Sopra candido vel cinta d'oliva
> Donna m'apparve, sotto verde manto,
> Vestita di color di fiamma viva.

Under a white veil encircled with olive, a lady appeared to
me, beneath a green mantle, clothed with colour of living
flame.

Dante describes how his heart knew the great
force of his old love, and the traces of the ancient
flame burst forth again at the sound of the voice
of his adorable lady, when she for this once only
addresses him by name, 'Dante, ben son, ben
son Beatrice' (Dante, I am, I am in truth
Beatrice).

But not yet is he safe, a flavour of much bitterness is mingled with her pity, and she at once
reminds him he must own his faults, and see his
errors before Lethe can be passed, and so she
proceeds in an earnest and forcible way to bring

before him his lapse from good intentions, his want of steadfastness, and his falling away from Divine Wisdom before she considers him fit to proceed further.

After Dante has been drawn through the waters of Lethe which wash away the memory of sin, and has drunk of Eunoë which brings back the memory of good, Beatrice conducts him up from the Terrestrial to the Heavenly Paradise.

LA VITA NUOVA

Before embarking upon the study of the *Divina Commedia* it is well to read the lovely little fantastic book written in Dante's early youth, which describes the first meeting with his beloved lady, when he and she were about nine years old, and contains many beautiful sonnets, of which perhaps the one written after his lady had been made a citizen of Heaven is the most beautiful:

> Beatrice is gone up into high Heaven,
> The Kingdom where the Angels are at peace;
> And lives with them; and to her friends is dead.

Not by the frost of winter was she driven
  Away, like others; nor by summer heats;
    But through a perfect gentleness, instead.
    For from the lamp of her meek lowlihood
Such an exceeding glory went up hence
  That it woke wonder in the Eternal Sire,
  Until a sweet desire
Entered Him for that lovely excellence,
  So that He bade her to Himself aspire;
Counting this weary and most evil place
Unworthy of a thing so full of grace.

                    D. G. ROSSETTI, transl.

Beautiful, too, are the lines in which he describes the effect which the mere sight of such a good and lovely woman had upon those around her:

My lady carries love within her eyes;
  All that she looks on is made pleasanter;
  Upon her path men turn to gaze at her;
He whom she greeteth feels his heart to rise,
And droops his troubled visage, full of sighs,
  And of his evil heart is then aware:
  Hate loves, and pride becomes a worshipper.
O women, help to praise her in somewise.
Humbleness, and the hope that hopeth well,
  By speech of hers into the mind are brought,
  And who beholds is blessèd oftenwhiles,
  The look she hath when she a little smiles
Cannot be said, nor holden in the thought;
'Tis such a new and gracious miracle.

                    D. G. ROSSETTI, transl.

Beatrice died, and Love wept within Dante's heart.

In glorious and regretful verse he says:

> Beyond the sphere which spreads to widest space
>   Now soars the sigh that my heart sends above: ·
>   A new perception born of grieving Love
> Guideth it upward the untrodden ways.
> When it hath reached unto the end, and stays,
>   It sees a lady round whom splendours move
>   In homage: till, by the great light thereof
> Abashed, the pilgrim spirit stands at gaze. . . .
>
> D. G. ROSSETTI, transl.

There came then into his mind that wonderful vision, and piercing the clouds of the darkness of this world, his spiritual sight seemed to show him his lady placed on a high seat in the great white rose of the Saints in bliss, and he sent his prayer up to God that he might write of her ' that which hath never been written of any other woman,' and surely his prayer was granted. Want of space prevents further lingering on the *Vita Nuova;* those who desire to read it can do so easily by procuring the little volume with English translation and Italian text side by side,

which has been brought out in the Temple
Classics series, or by perusing the beautiful
translation of Dante Gabriel Rossetti. For
Italian readers the excellent editions by Scherillo
or Barbi are recommended.

LA DIVINA COMMEDIA

The word. *Comœdia*, or *Commedia*, was given
to his poem by Dante himself as it ends happily,
in contrast to tragic poems, which terminate in
gloom and sadness. The word *Divina* was
added later.

CONSTRUCTION

The *Divina Commedia* is the most beautiful
book produced in the middle ages, and no one
can read it without recognising the deep religious feeling pervading the whole work. But
the courtesy and refinement shown, even in the
most weird parts, and undoubtedly running
throughout the poem, is often unnoticed in view
of strange, forcible passages not acceptable in
our more delicate age.

Something must be said as to the form of this great poem. In its very simplicity it is perfect in design, and adheres to a precise and definite theory based upon the number three and its multiples. The number three was a mystical number with the Romans, and came to be regarded as even more sacred after the introduction of Christianity, when the conception of the Holy Trinity developed.

The poem is divided into three parts—the *Inferno*, the *Purgatorio*, and the *Paradiso*—each of these divisions having nine gradations of descent or ascent, or three times three. Each portion consists of thirty-three Cantos, with one placed at the commencement as an introduction ; this makes one hundred in all, thus completing the perfect number, ten times ten.

Written in the Italian terza rima, it consists of three lines each holding in general eleven syllables, but in certain instances this rule is departed from, and there are either less or more feet to a line, the rhythm then depends upon the accentuation and emphasis in the pronunciation. This variety produces the plasticity of metre

which, when well balanced, goes so far to pro-
cure beauty of style. The wit and humour of
the writer, his love of colour, light, and sound,
together with his minute notice of the workings
of nature in earth and sky, all tend to such a
sense of movement that the strictness of the
rhyme does not obtrude itself.

An instance of the 'tronco' or cut-off line is

'Dell' opera che mal per te si fe,'

whilst

'E s'una entrava, un' altra n'uscia fuori'

represents the *sdrucciolo* or gliding form : and

'Nel mezzo del cammin di nostra vita'

is the normal line with eleven feet.

The terza rima, or rhyme in stanzas of three
lines, is carried on throughout by the central line
always rhyming with the first and third lines of
the next stanza.

At the commencement of a Canto, line *one* and
three rhyme only with each other, line *two*, the
middle line, being the leading one to be followed
in *four* and *six*, line *five* beginning a fresh termination.

Thus, in *Purgatorio* xxviii, 1, we find :

1 Vago già di cercar dentro e dintor*no*
2   La divina foresta spessa e vi*va*,
3   Ch'agli occhi temperava il nuovo gior*no,*
4 Senza più aspettar, lasciai la ri*va*,
5   Prendendo la campagna lento len*to*
6   Su per lo suol che d'ogni parte oli*va.*
7 Un' aura dolce, senza mutamen*to*
8   Avere in sè, mi feria per la fron*te*
9   Non di più colpo che soave ven*to ;*
10 Per cui le fronde, tremolando pron*te,*
11   Tutte quante piegavano alla par*te*
12   U' la prim 'ombra gitta il santo mon*te ;*

.   .   .   .

and so on to the end of each canto which ter-
minates in a single line called a 'ritornello';
this rhymes only with the middle line of the
preceding stanza and makes the number of lines
complete.

The best way to arrive at a true knowledge of
the Italian of this great poem, and so to appreciate
the beauty of language and ideas, is to translate
each word into English as simply and literally as
may be possible.   Much of the elegance is lost
by a loose or careless rendering, for this Italian is
one of the few examples of poetry in which there
are no superfluous words.

C

Care and study, with attention paid to small words bearing many meanings, will be well rewarded.

No English translation can reach or touch the exquisite metre of the Italian terza rima; our language possesses too few double-syllable words rhyming with each other to make it possible to carry on the metre after the Italian fashion with any very successful result. Sometimes one, sometimes another translation seems to give the best clue to Dante's meaning.

The Text

Experts only can fitly deal with the Text, but it is probable that the first copies of Dante's work, intended for the best of his friends, were illuminated and adorned by himself with some of those beautiful capitals and miniatures which are generally to be found in the books of the thirteenth and fourteenth century, before the art of printing was invented.

That Dante was an artist is known by the reference in the *Vita Nuova* to his paintings of angels, and in *Purgatorio* vii he gives a list of the actual pigments (so Ruskin declares) which were used in illuminating, an art he must have well understood :

Gold and fine silver and cochineal, and white lead, and Indian wood serene and lucid, and fresh emerald just broken, would have been excelled, as less by greater, by the flowers and grass of the place.

The word *illuminare* was first used by Dante to designate this art, so in speaking of these illuminated MSS. we are employing the term invented by him when writing his great poem.

The original title-pages and autographs of all Dante's works seem to have disappeared, a most unfortunate loss, and no trace of his signature, nor a scrap of his writing appears now to be extant, notwithstanding the fact of his having been a foremost citizen, and having carried through important official negotiations for his native city.

Cary, however, refers to a belief existing about one hundred years ago that a specimen of Dante's handwriting was then to be found in a manuscript at Gubbio, on a sonnet to Busone, one of those friends who gave the poet shelter in his exile. Perhaps it is there still.

There is a framed sonnet shown with pride by the custodian in the Palazzo dei Console at Gubbio bearing at the top the words 'Dante a Busone,' but the rhyme is poor, and the evidence so small as to its authenticity that experts throw discredit upon it. Dante is believed to have stayed both at the town and country houses of Busone, and also at a Convent in the neighbourhood. The theory that the poet took an amanuensis about with him during the long years of his wandering exile and did not write with his own hand is untenable. Further research in the other libraries at Gubbio and Fonte Avellana might bring something more to light.

Boccaccio speaks in his day of the existence of various epistles, and Leonardo Aretino (d. 1444) in his *Vita di Dante* says: 'Dilettossi di musica, e di suoni; e di sua mano egregiamente disegnava. Fù ancora scrittore perfetto, ed era la lettera sua magra e lunga, e molto corretta, secondo io ho veduto in alcune pistole di sua propria mano scritto.'

We can imagine the long artistic characters, thin and gracefully formed with precision and correctness, since the following is the meaning of the passage. 'He delighted in music and sound, and drew skilfully with his own hand. He was besides a perfect scribe, the characters being thin and long and very correct, according to what I (Leonardo) have seen in some epistles written by Dante's own hand.' The bewildering discrepancies and alterations in the text of the *Divina Commedia* are due to the fact that in Dante's day printing had not been invented, and authors were obliged to trust to a multitude of inaccurate copyists who followed the trade to make a livelihood, as in Dr Witte's often quoted instance of the man who made one hundred copies in order to provide dowries for his daughters.

This slipshod fashion of copying, and the licence taken with the text, is the cause of much of the dissension which arises over the meaning of certain passages, for even the omission of a comma will affect the gist of a sentence, and the substitution of one letter of the alphabet for another will entirely obscure or alter the meaning.

The fact that it was written in Italian and not Latin added to the difficulty of copying. Experts say that no manuscripts of a date earlier than 1335 or 1336, *i.e.* about fifteen years after the poet's death, can now be found. Between 500 and 600 copies exist still, hardly any of them are identical, so the classifying and arranging of these precious works is a huge undertaking.

There are in Florence alone more than 200 MS. copies, twenty-seven from the fine Ashburnham Collection having now gone over to the Laurentian Library. The earliest known miniature of the poet is to be found in the Riccardiana Library.

Rome ranks next with over fifty Codices, some of the most precious being in the Vatican Library, one of which contains the celebrated dedicatory letter of Boccaccio to Petrarch.

Perugia guards amongst her treasures two manuscripts of vast interest, fondly believed by the custodian to be contemporary work, but at any rate they date from no later than the middle of the fourteenth century. One is a copy of the *Inferno* only, with the most fascinating double-

Dante assailed by wild beasts, and rescued by Virgil.

From a XIVth Century Codex.

Tilli, Perugia.

[*To face p.* 38.

page illustration. It is in tones of grey, except that the poet has a deep blue robe and cap which have kept the colour for all these centuries.

Dante is shown asleep in the 'selva selvaggia'; his awakening to see the three beasts and his efforts to elude them are amusing. When on the second page he turns from the open jaws of one beast whose head just appears round the corner, and he holds out his hands with despairing gestures to Virgil, the effect is lifelike; then the hurrying figure following his rescuer up the hill completes this well-drawn mediæval picture.

The other old MS. is a complete copy with quaint illustrations. Both manuscripts are written in beautifully small characters, and contain a number of minute marginal notes and occasional corrections of the text.

Siena possesses valuable copies of the *Divina Commedia* in the Biblioteca Comunale, and amongst her state Archives in the Palazzo Piccolomini are arranged thirty-three old documents dealing with persons who are mentioned in the poem, such as a compact between the Ghibellines of Florence (the principal of whom was Farinata) and the Comune of Siena; a bull of Boniface VIII releasing from excommunication ecclesiastics who had paid over church moneys for secular purposes; a note of a fine which Casella had to pay for wandering about the city at night; the codicil to Sapia's will, and the deliberations of the Council General as to the search for the waters of Diana.

The interest to Dante students is great. It is a thrilling moment when the old Guardian in the Library places in one's hand an ancient book which he is re-binding, and asserts that it might have been pored over by the great poet himself in those far-off days.

Copies of the Manuscript can be found also in Milan, Turin, Venice, Naples, Bologna, Ravenna, Palermo, Vicenza, Piacenza, Modena, Cortina, Udine, Paris, Vienna, Berlin, Stuttgart, Copenhagen, &c.

We possess a fine collection in England, 17 at the British Museum, 14 at the Bodleian (Oxford), 3 at Cambridge, 1 at Eton, 3 at Cheltenham, 6 belong to the Earl of Leicester at Holkham,

1 at Glasgow, besides those in Lord Vernon's library and in other private libraries. A fourteenth century MS. in the British Museum has beautiful illuminated letters, and at the commencement of the *Inferno* Dante is depicted at a desk, his cap and robe are blue, his sleeves and collar red. In the *Purgatorio* Virgil and Dante are to be seen in a boat, and in the *Paradiso* Dante is represented with arms folded reverently addressing Beatrice. An unpublished Commentary in the British Museum by Serravalle, Bishop of Fermo, is of great interest to English people as it is the sole authority for Dante's visit to England and Oxford, the statement being found in the 5th Preambulum. This Commentary was composed during the Council in Constance, A.D. 1417, at the instance of Cardinal Amidei and Nicholas Bubwith, Bishop of Bath and Wells, and Robert Hallam, Bishop of Salisbury.

The printed texts of the *Divina Commedia* are legion, some being magnificent tomes. The fine first edition of Cristoforo Landino (1480), with illustrations by Botticelli, is of great value, a copy having recently been carried off from

London to America for £2000. At much less
cost copies of the issue of 1564, with Commentary
by Landino and Vellutello, may be picked up in
old book shops. For ordinary reading the good
texts of editions with short Italian notes by
Torraca, Casini, or B. Bianchi are very useful,
but as the most generally excellent text Dr
Moore considers that of Dr Witte of Berlin to
hold quite an exceptional position among all
editions ancient and modern.

For the entire collection of Dante's works we
have to thank Dr Moore, who has published at
the Oxford Press a most careful and scholarly
edition in small compass, embodying the best
readings, and containing the *Credo* which tradition
says was composed by Dante in order to silence
the awkward questionings of an Inquisitor who
suspected him of holding non-Catholic opinions.

Many are the illustrators of the *Divina Commedia*, which lends itself to such varied treatment; Botticelli however drew some of the
finest illustrations, which thanks to a German
firm have been reproduced so as to be within
the reach of those who desire to possess them.

DANTE'S ERUDITION

The immense range of Dante's knowledge is
dwelt upon in a little brochure by Dr Cossio,
who draws attention to the fact that he 'was
no mean theologian, having studied the Latin
fathers. His philosophy was derived from the
writings of Aristotle, S. Thomas Aquinas, Boethius, &c. His knowledge of grammar, logic,
rhetoric, arithmetic, music, geometry, and astro-
nomy, together with the Latin classics, Italian
dialects, and international law, was profound.'
There are, according to Dr Moore, in the *Divina
Commedia* 500 quotations from the Bible (the
Vulgate), 300 from Aristotle, 200 from Virgil.
Much skill is shown in his minute architectural
arrangement of the *Inferno*, and an archæological
bent comes out in the enumeration of buildings
and bridges in old Florence, as well as basilicas
in Rome, whilst his love for natural beauties
does not let him forget to mention the Vatican
gardens, and Mt. Uccellatoio near Florence,
places where he probably loved to roam and
unbend his mind, rejoicing in the sunshine, the

glory of the flowers, and the songs of birds, those
feathered songsters who must often have been
his only companions during his solitary wanderings through the Casentino and many other parts
of Italy.

DANTE'S LOVE FOR BIRDS

It may be opportune here to notice that the
love of Dante for birds is very remarkable, and
in his mention of them he constantly refers to
some old legend about them. He must have
studied their habits most minutely. Look at the
lines in *Pur.* ix, 13–18, when describing the
Swallow early dawn and the ways of the melancholy little
'rondinella.' 'The hour in which the swallow
begins to tune her sad complaint near morning
in memory perchance of her first sorrows, and
when our soul more a stranger to the flesh and
less a prisoner of thought, is, as it were, divinely
free for her visions.' The allusion is to the
fable of Progne having been changed into a
swallow.

When quoting this passage and giving his
translation Mr J. A. Symonds remarks 'that the

power of holding deep thought and evanescent feelings in solution, and of connecting them with some well-defined scene, some accurately noted moment, is granted only to poetry of the highest order, and this power is eminent in the above celebrated passage. What is noticeable in these lines is the mixture of accurate observation and description with far-reaching speculation, and the exquisite phrasing by which different thoughts are merged and made to form one element.' Much the same may be said of the following passage, *Par.* xxiii, 1.

> Even as a bird, 'mid the beloved leaves,
>   Quiet upon the nest of her sweet brood
>   Throughout the night, that hideth all things from us,
> Who, that she may behold their longed-for looks
>   And find the food wherewith to nourish them,
>   In which, to her, grave labours grateful are,
> Anticipates the time on open spray
>   And with an ardent longing waits the sun,
>   Gazing intent as soon as breaks the dawn.
>   LONGFELLOW, transl.

The translation of the well-known lines describing the singing of the Lark will be found in the chapter on the *Paradiso :*

Lark

Qual lodoletta che in aere si spazia
Prima cantando, e poi tace contenta
Dell' ultima dolcezza che la sazia.

Par. xx, 73.

Doves   The affection of Turtle-doves is noted in re-
lating the incident of Francesca and Paolo in
Inf. v, 82, how, 'called onward by desire and
a strong affectionate appeal, they fly with open
and steady wing to the sweet nest.' Then again
in *Pur.* ii, 124, the sudden haste with which they
leave their food if startled when feeding. And
further in *Par.* xxv, 19, the loving actions of the
great saints S. James and S. Peter are likened to
'those of a Dove who alights near to his com-
panion, and with murmurings and circlings they
pour forth their affection one to the other.'

Starlings   The sad spirits in the second Circle of the
Inferno (v, 40) are described as blown along by
a bitter blast, 'di qua, di là, di giù, di su,' like
Starlings carried away on their wings in large
and crowded troops during the cold weather,
since they are some of the earliest birds to leave
the shelter of trees and come forth into the open
to find worms in the early spring.

'As the Cranes,' says Dante, 'go chanting their Cranes
lays, making of themselves a long streak in the
air, so I saw shadows, uttering wailing sounds
carried away by this strife of winds.'—*Inf.* v, 46.

The migratory habits of Cranes who fly off,
some to the mountains, some to the sands, the
first shy of the frost, and the second of the sun,
are touched upon in *Pur.* xxvi, 43.

In *Paradiso* xix, 91, a few lovely lines describe Storks
the care and devotion of the mother Stork who
'right above her nest sweeps round when she
has fed her brood, and as the one to whom she
has given food looks up at her, so did the blessed
image (the Eagle) ply its wings which were
driven by many counsels,' and so did Dante
admiringly and in humility lift up his brow to
gaze.   The noise which Storks make with their
beaks is mentioned in *Inf.* xxxii, 36.

Dante was very fond of Falconry, a sport Falcons
much in vogue in his day, and his keen knowledge is frequently shown in this poem :

> My gaze pursued intently
> As my eye pursues a Falcon flying.
> *Par.* xviii, 44.

The pride which the bird takes in its appearance is noted :

> Like the Falcon, who issuing from the hood, moves its head and claps its wings, wishing to show its will and make itself beautiful.—*Par.* xix, 34.

The anger at defeat which a Falcon shows when a Duck suddenly dives down into the water and eludes him.—*Inf.* xxii, 130.

The weary discontent of a Falcon when he has found no prey : 'As the Falcon who has been long upon the wing without seeing lure or bird, makes the Falconer call out : 'Ah! thou stoopest,' descends weary, then quickly sweeps round in many a circle and places himself far away from his master, disdainful and sullen.'—*Inf.* xvii, 127.

Dante points out that a lesson is to be learnt from the habits of Falcons and Hawks :

> Smite earth with thy heels,
> Thine eyes lift upward to the lure, that whirls
> The eternal King with revolutions vast,
> Even as the Hawk that first his feet surveys,
> Then turns him to the call and stretches forward,
> Through the desire of food that draws him thither. . . .
> *Pur.* xix, 64 : LONGFELLOW, transl.

Surely towards the end of winter we must
often think of the Blackbird who tempted Provi-
dence, as the saying is, and at the first breath of
warmer air flew off from a snug winter home, his
hurried desire for spring, and recklessness, being
the cause of the Italian proverb which says that
the Blackbird cries out at the end of January:
' I fear Thee no more, O Lord, now the winter is
behind me.'   Sapia presumed upon her evil wish
being fulfilled, and cried to God,

> ' Omai più non ti temo !'
> Come fa il merlo per poca bonaccia.
> *Pur.* xiii, 122.

> So that I lifted upward my bold face
>   Crying to God, ' Henceforth I fear thee not,'
> As did the blackbird at the little sunshine.

The habit of Rooks to come out in the early
dawn and warm their cold glistening feathers by
taking short or long flights in the air is remarked
upon in *Par.* xxi, 35.

Note the description in *Pur.* xxiv, 64, of the
flights of ' birds that winter along the Nile, sometimes flying in the air in squadrons, or close

companies, then flying in greater haste in file, or single lines.'

> And as birds from river banks
> Arisen, now in round, now lengthen'd troop,
> Array them in their flight, greeting, as seems,
> Their new found pastures; so within the lights,
> The saintly creatures flying; sang; and made
> Now D, now I, now L, figured i' the air.
> *Par.* xviii, 73 : CARY, transl.

Eagle The Imperial Eagle, the bird of Jove, is naturally not passed over by the Poet.

The great company of 'those lords of the highest song' (the poets of antiquity) is likened to an Eagle which soars above the rest in *Inf.* iv, 94.

The glorious plumage, lofty mien and keen vision possessed by the golden-feathered Eagle comes (*Pur.* ix, 19) to Dante as in a dream, when Lucia carries him up to the three steps before the gate of *Purgatorio.*

Notice of the Eagle standard of Constantine is to be found in *Par.* vi, 1, whilst in *Pur.* xxxii, 112, there is a vivid description of the symbolical descent of Jove's bird upon the mystic

Car of the Church, and of the destruction wrought by its terrific attacks.

At the entrance to *Paradiso* (*Par*. i, 46) Beatrice stands gazing on the sun 'more fixedly than any Eagle.'

Finally the magnificent description of the figure of an Eagle shown forth when the planet Jove is reached in *Par*. xviii is amazing in its brilliance. More than a thousand lights pricked out in gold on the silver surface of the planet served to form its head, while each separate soul burnt like a ruby. The most brilliant lights in the eye and eyebrows are described as being the souls of the greatest of earth's sovereign rulers, who in a body formed this emblematical figure of righteous judgment.

PART II

DELL' INFERNO

Descent of Christ into Limbo.
Fra Angelico.

Anderson, Rome.

[*To face p.* 54.

DELL' INFERNO

Se tu segui tua stella,
Non puoi fallire a glorioso porto.
Inf. xv, 55.

If thou thy star do follow
Thou canst not fail thee of a glorious port.

Chè, seggendo in piuma in fama non si vien.
Inf. xxiv, 47.

He who sits in feather beds shall not come to fame.

ANTE himself helps us to under-
stand the object of his writings, for
speaking of his *Commedia* in a letter
said to be written to Can Grande
(*Epistola* x) he remarks : 'Let us
consider the subject of this work according to the
letter first and then according to the allegorical
meaning. The subject of the whole work taken
literally is the state of souls after death regarded
as a matter of fact : for the action of the whole
work deals with this and is about this. But if
the work be taken allegorically its subject is Man,

55

in so far as by merit or demerit in the exercise of free will he is exposed to the rewards or punishments of justice. The object of the whole work is to make those who live in this life leave their state of misery, and to lead them to a state of happiness. . . . The poem is of many senses discoverable by four methods of interpretation—Literal, Allegorical, Moral and Anagogical (or Mystical).'

This being so, can we wonder it has been said: 'What a man brings to Dante's poems *that* he finds there?'

The Inferno—this powerful and splendid portion of the *Divina Commedia*—opens with the well-known words, 'nel mezzo del cammin di nostra vita' (midway upon the journey of our life), and they lead us to consider what Dante's age was when he wrote his famous poem. He probably commenced it in early or middle life, with all the force of his energy in full swing; he finished it during his closing years amongst the pine woods of Ravenna. The last thirteen cantos of the *Paradiso* are said to have been found hidden in the wall of the house which he inhabited, but not until the search had been considered hopeless by his sons Pietro and Jacopo. To the latter (it is related) Dante appeared in a dream, and, after explaining that he was still alive, granted Jacopo's request by pointing to a window-seat in which next day the missing pages were found all mildewed and well-nigh illegible. They were copied and thus the great work was made complete for posterity.

Benvenuto da Imola in his Commentary quotes an Arabian saying : ' It is good to sift a measure of sand to find a pearl,' and notes how Dante carries out the idea by describing the arduous hunt for the pearl in the *Purgatorio*, the joyful finding of the pearl of great price in the *Paradiso*, whilst the horrors of the *Inferno* are intended to dispose men's minds to go in search of it. The *Inferno* contains a stupendous warning to mankind as to what may be expected to follow sin indulged—especially the guilt of 'accidia,' or utter slothfulness in not rising up to fight the temptations which beset each human being—the sinful folly of not looking for the Light which does shine in the heart of the most benighted, that spark of the Divine nature which points to the 'glorioso porto,' and enables happiness and fame to be grasped : without which Light 'whoso consumes his life leaves such vestige of himself on earth as smoke in air, or foam in water.'—*Inf.* xxiv, 51.

A brief list is here given of the sins punished in each circle of the *Inferno*, without the subdivisions which are many. Readers can work out the scheme for themselves. Suffice it to say that the shape of the *Inferno* is described as that of a cone with the point turned downwards, the upper circles are the largest and as it nears the bottom it contracts, leaving room for only one figure—Lucifer.

PLAN OF THE INFERNO

The vestibule	Those who lived for naught but themselves	Canto III
Circle I Limbo	The unbaptized	Canto IV
Circle II	The Carnal	Canto V
Circle III	The Gluttonous	Canto VI
Circle IV	The Avaricious and Prodigal	Canto VII
Circle V	The Wrathful and Sullen	Canto VII
Circle VI	Heretics (City of Dis)	Canto VIII
Circle VII	The Violent	Canto XII
Circle VIII	The Fraudulent	Canto XVIII
Circle IX	Traitors	Canto XXXI

. . . Il vermo reo che il mondo fora.

Inf. xxxiv, 108.

(The fell worm who mines the world.)

Over the shoulder of the arch-traitor, Virgil guides Dante to grope his way and thus issue out 'to see again the stars' on Easter Even, this terrible journey having occupied twenty-five hours. The *Inferno* abounds with very beautiful and graphic descriptions set amongst a mass of strange, weird and mediæval detail, not always happy to dwell upon. It is to the better known subjects that I desire to draw attention.

Here at the outset let me state that no excuse will be made for treating this great poem as a *real* vision. The true poetic genius of Dante carries one away, as perforce it should do, and it is only to those who give full rein to their own imagination that understanding will be vouchsafed, and Dante will enter into their souls. They who seek aright shall find.

Beginners who prosaically cavil and question every small point, and exercise no imagination, will not be likely to come to a true and wide knowledge of the meaning of the *Divina Commedia*. It is by reason of their imaginative insight that the authors of the *Introduction to the Study of Dante*,[1] *Dante's Commedia—its Scope*

[1] J. Addington Symonds (A. & C. Black).

and Value,[1] *Dante et la philosophie Catholique au treizième Siècle*,[2] and *Dante's Ten Heavens*,[3] should above others be first studied. Help may be found in consulting Longfellow's translation with the valuable notes,[4] or the text and translation side by side in the Temple Edition.[5] Afterwards the more critical and argumentative books may be assimilated, since learned students love to spend their time in most minute enquiries and researches concerning the different texts, readings, and historical allusions, thus bringing within reach of thousands a vast store of interesting detail to which they would otherwise be debarred access.

It has been pointed out by one clever student that study of this poem should commence with the second Canto of the *Paradiso*, and there is something to be said for this advice as the Canto is beautiful enough to tempt further research. But since the contrast between darkness and

[1] Hettinger, trans. by Henry S. Bowden (Burns & Oates).
[2] Frédéric Ozanam (Libr. Victor Lecoffre, Paris).
[3] Edmund G. Gardner (Constable & Co.).
[4] Longfellow's translation with notes (George Routledge & Sons).
[5] Temple Classics (Dent & Co.).

light, and the description of the gradual rising upwards through the three realms shows most consummate art, it is needful to commence study at the beginning of the *Inferno* in order to grasp the procession, scope, and meaning of the work.

Let me add, however, one note of caution. At the first feeling of weariness let the readers look up again to behold the stars, and, understanding a little of the gist of the pages, turn resolutely to peruse the *Purgatorio* and *Paradiso*, until soothed by the beautiful thoughts and rhythmic lines they feel able and desirous to renew their explorations in the gloomy Infernal regions.

Too often readers go no further than a few of the first Cantos, become determined that Dante is a vindictive man, writing with no other intent than to place his enemies in Hell, throw the book aside, and thus never reach the finest parts of the poem. We will not regret the passionate and vehement invectives hurled against his enemies in righteous indignation, for we cannot wonder at the bitterness which Dante felt towards his treacherous fellow-citizens, since his noble en-

deavour to hold the balance of justice between the
Neri and Bianchi factions was one of the immediate
causes of his exile from his beloved Florence.

It must ever be borne in mind that all the
personages introduced into the *Divina Commedia*
are typical either of great sinners, repentant
sinners, or saints : and although it is true that
he places many of his personal enemies and contemporaries in very hot, cold, or terrible places,
a large number of these representative people
are 'those known to fame' in past history, such
as Brutus, Cassius, Caiaphas, Judas, Ulysses
and Diomed, Hector and Achilles, Semiramis,
Cleopatra, Nimrod, Attila, and many more against
whom he could have had no personal spite.
Surely he does but echo the Psalmist, ' Do not
I hate them, O Lord, that hate Thee, and am
not I grieved with those that rise up against
Thee ? Yea, I hate them right sore, even as
though they were mine enemies.'

This aspect of Dante's meaning, his fervent
jealousy for God's glory, and hatred of sinners
as those who transgress His laws, is too often
lost sight of.

Vestibule

Following the journey of the two travellers through the gloomy portal designed by the Justice, Power, Wisdom and Love of its Divine Maker, we find Dante very much troubled at being amongst the dolorous company of those who have 'lost the good of their intellect,' that is, the revealed knowledge of God, and he only feels a little comfort when Virgil puts his hand upon his and with cheerful countenance exhorts him to lay aside distrustful cowardice and to follow bravely.

The air was filled with strange sounds, high and hoarse voices breathing forth words of anger or sorrow made a great tumult, rendered more terrible by reason of the lurid light which shone as it were through a dust-storm. Here the fallen angels chased from Heaven, and those people who lived on earth for nothing but themselves without any hope or endeavour to do right, were swept along across a wide plain in perpetual wretchedness.

The sad river of Acheron is soon reached

across which the crowds of souls are piloted. Then, rendered senseless by the violent wind and blinding red light, Dante falls to the ground. When roused by loud thunder he finds himself on the other side of the river looking down into the dark valley.

Limbo
Circle I

Virgil's face was white, not with fear but with pity, as he entered the First Circle or Limbo. Here there was no noise nor sound of anything but sighs, which made the air tremble, coming from those unbaptized ones who, living before Christ, did not worship God aright.

' And of these am I myself,' says Virgil.

His sad lament over his own lot is most pathetic, he calls attention to his state and that of other people in Limbo with these words:

> Thou dost not ask
> What spirits these, which thou beholdest, are?
> Now will I have thee know, ere thou go farther,
> That they sinned not; and if they merit had,
> 'Tis not enough, because they had not baptism
> Which is the portal of the Faith thou holdest;
> And if they were before Christianity,
> In the right manner they adored not God;
> And among such as these am I myself,

For such defects, and not for other guilt,
Lost are we, and are only so far punished,
That without hope we live on in desire.

Inf. iv, 31 : LONGFELLOW, transl.

Much sorrow entered into Dante's heart as he listened, and he then began to ask Virgil the question as to whether any ever went forth from this spot either by their own merit or that of others, and Virgil replies :

Io era nuovo in questo stato,
Quando ci vidi venire un possente
Con segno di vittoria coronato.
Trasseci l'ombra del primo parente,
D'Abel suo figlio, e quella di Noè,
Di Moisè legista e ubbidiente ;
Abraam patriarca, e David re,
Israel con lo padre, e co' suoi nati,
E con Rachele, per cui tanto fe',
Ed altri molti ; e faceli beati :
E vo' che sappi che, dinanzi ad essi,
Spiriti umani non eran salvati.

Inf. iv, 52–63.

I was new to that estate when I saw a Mighty One arrive amongst us, crowned with the sign of victory. He drew forth the shade of our first parent, of Abel his son, and that of Noah, of Moses the legislator and obedient one; the patriarch Abraham, and David the King, Israel with his father, and his

E

children, with Rachel for whom he did so much, and many others, and made them blessed. And I will you to know, that before these no human spirits were saved.

Those readers who have seen Fra Angelico's paintings in S. Marco at Florence will be immediately reminded of the quaint and suggestive little fresco to be found there, depicting the Descent into Hades of the Victorious Crowned One. A copy of it is placed as a frontispiece to this short notice of the *Inferno*, by reason of the beauty of the idea and its appropriateness to these lines, which are met with on reaching the place where Virgil was stationed in Limbo when implored by Beatrice to go to Dante's rescue.

The radiant glorious figure of the Light of Life penetrating into the dark abyss where the souls were held in bondage, and drawing them out, brings before us and teaches what Dante certainly meant to imply, that it is He only Who can overcome all difficulties and free souls from error and darkness. These rescued souls are 'those who believed in Christ to come' according to *Par.* xxxii, 24, and therefore in the description of the Paradiso they are pictured by the Poet as filling one half of the petals of the White Rose of the Saints in bliss, while to those who lived after Christ is allotted the other half. (*Par.* xxxii, 27.)

The travellers proceed through a wood to fields where they are met by the great ancient poets, who are pointed out by 'the good Master' to be headed by Homer, Horace, Ovid, and Lucan.

> Così vid' io adunar la bella scuola
> Di quel signor dell' altissimo canto,
> Che sopra gli altri com' aquila vola.
> *Inf.* iv, 94.

> Thus I beheld assemble the fair school
> Of that lord of the song pre-eminent,
> Who o'er the others like an eagle soars.
> LONGFELLOW, transl.

Virgil smiled upon Dante when, upon explaining who the stranger was, the courteous poets asked him to join them, and he paced along making the sixth of the illustrious group. The rest of this canto contains a long list of celebrated people well known in ancient history and the drama.

The First Steps

Circle
II

Virgil and Dante then descend to the second Circle where Carnal Sinners are placed in the *Inferno* proper. No words of mine can describe the wonderful sympathy and pathos shown by the poet in Canto v when he records his meeting with the sobbing, wind-driven shades of Francesca da Rimini and Paolo, who, 'like Turtle-doves called onward by desire, with open and steady wings fly to the sweet nest through the air by their volition; thus came they from the land where Dido is, approaching us athwart the air malign, so strong was the affectionate appeal.'

Guido da Polenta, Lord of Ravenna and cousin (as some historians say) of Francesca, had been very good to the Poet, giving him an asylum in his exile, so no doubt he knew the story well and felt intensely what this tragedy meant to his friends. Carlyle, in his book on Hero Worship, speaking of Francesca says: ' I suppose if ever pity as a mother's was in the heart of a man it was in Dante's. But a man

who has not known rigour cannot pity either.
His very pity will be cowardly egoistic senti-
mentality or little better. I know not in the
world an affection equal to that of Dante. It
is a tenderness, a trembling, longing, pitying
love, like the wail of an Æolian harp, soft, soft,
like a child's young heart, and then that stern,
sore shadowed heart! These longings of his
towards Beatrice, their meeting together in *Purgatorio*, his gazing on her pure transfigured eyes,
her, that had been purified by death so long, sepa-
rated from him so far. One likens it to the song
of angels, it is amongst the purest utterances of
affection, perhaps the very purest that ever came
out of a human soul.' It is curious to think that
these words come from the heart of the stern
Carlyle and allude to Dante, who by many is
supposed likewise to have been a very stern
man; they must both have been gifted with great
insight and sympathy so as to be able to form
a truer estimate of mankind than those who think
less deeply, and show their feelings more on the
surface. This celebrated passage is too well
known to be dwelt upon here, a tale of world-

wide renown, and old—ah! old as the hills. It contains the lines (121, 123):

> Nessun maggior dolore
> Che ricordarsi del tempo felice
> Nella miseria.

> There is no greater sorrow
> Than to be mindful of the happy time
> In misery.
>
> LONGFELLOW, transl.

which are referred to by Tennyson when he says :

> This is truth the Poet sings,
> That a sorrow's crown of sorrows is remembering happier things.

Pierced to the heart by the bitter wailing of these sadly loving souls clinging to each other in the misty gloom, Dante's grief overpowers him and he swoons to the ground.

There will be no attempt to follow the kaleidoscopic descriptions of scenes and places in the gloomy abyss of the *Inferno,* nor to recount the endless procession of spirits recognised or mentioned in each round; people of every nation and tongue, from poets of antiquity in Limbo on past

the 8th Bolgia of Circle viii, in which Pope
Boniface VIII was soon expected to take his place
amongst the evil counsellors, down to where the
three arch-traitors were placed in the lowest
depths, since our main object is to notice specially
beautiful passages.

A Rapid Survey

At the return of consciousness after his interview with Francesca, Dante hurries along
through the hail, rain and snow pouring upon
those spirits overcome by gluttony, only recognising one, Ciacco, who gives him information
about the fate of some foremost Florentine
citizens.

Circle III

Virgil here suggests in answer to Dante's
questioning that even fallen souls may gradually
increase their knowledge of the difference between
good and evil. (*Inf.* vi, 107.)

The avaricious and prodigal in two companies
roll great weights against each other around the
two halves of the fourth Circle. Virgil says they
cannot be recognised since evil-giving and evil-

Circle IV

saving have blunted their faculties, made them indistinguishable, and deprived them of the bright world. (*Inf.* vii, 58.)

Circle V

Loitering being forbidden, Dante and his guide make a quick journey to the stream forming the dark marsh in which the wrathful souls are punished, and where sullen sobbing ones who, having looked with gloomy thoughts upon life in God's beautiful world, were overcome by 'accidioso fummo' (sloth-producing vapours), here meet their deserts. Ferried across in a boat which is the heavier for Dante's weight, they pass the violent Florentine Filippo Argenti, so named because he had his horses shod with silver. The red towers and walls of a town now appear, but on reaching the gate more than a thousand rebellious angels bar their entrance.

Then follows a typical instance of the allegorical meaning which pervades the whole of this poem.

Man, in the person of Dante, approaches the gates with a desire to gain knowledge of the punishment of heresy; Reason, represented by Virgil, advises him to halt, but goes on himself

to parley with the caitiff crew of unbelievers.
He is baffled by their arguments and mockery.
Evil consciences, like Furies, threaten to call up
the Head of Medusa—Doubt—which turns men's
minds into stone. The action of Virgil in cover-
ing Dante's eyes may mean lawful authority
condemning the publishing of heretical and bad
books.

Reason remains undecided, until the memory
that help from on high had been promised by
Beatrice enables Virgil to look for the coming
of the Angel, who, with a mighty sound sweeping down all opposition, crosses the passage of
the Styx with dry feet. (*Inf.* ix, 81.)

THE CITY OF DIS

After the Messenger from heaven, bearing in
his right hand a wand and with his left waving
off the heavy vapour, had opened the gate of the
fell City of Dis (Canto ix, 89), an extraordinary
sight is described as meeting the eyes of Dante
and Virgil, there where the arch-heretics meet
their bitter punishment. The entire centre of

Circle
VI

the ground was covered with sepulchres, just such as may be seen to this day at Arles, where the country centuries ago was honeycombed with tombs and where many square stone ones, some five feet or more in height with heavy lids, made in Roman times, are still in good preservation.

The legends of ancient days which tell that Charlemagne's warriors were buried there after Roncesvalles, and also tales of the battle of Aleschans, or Alyscamps, when the defeat of Christians by Saracens took place, must have been in Dante's mind when he refers in the following lines to Arles. At Pola too, an old seaport on the Adriatic, are still to be found the remains of a large Roman Amphitheatre. Tradition says that Dante stayed at the Abbey of S. Michele in Monte a short distance eastward of Pola, between which and the abbey there then existed a vast cemetery. Traces of that have disappeared, and a fortress now stands on the site of the Abbey which was in ruins in 1845; but fragments of tombs with pagan inscriptions are still found in the rough walls dividing the fields in that part of the country.

Sì com' ad Arli, ove Rodano stagna,
    Sì com' a Pola presso del Quarnaro,
    Che Italia chiude e suoi termini bagna,
Fanno i sepolcri tutto il loco varo,
    Così facevan quivi d'ogni parte,
    Salvo che il modo v'era più amaro.

Inf. ix, 112.

Even as at Arles, where stagnant grows the Rhone,
    Even as at Pola near to the Quarnaro,
    That shuts in Italy and bathes its borders,
The sepulchres make all the place uneven;
    So likewise did they there on every side,
    Saving that there the manner was more bitter;
For flames between the sepulchres were scattered,
    By which they so intensely heated were,
    That iron more so asks not any art.

LONGFELLOW, transl.

The great Ghibelline Chief Farinata rose out of one of these tombs uprearing his head and breast 'as if he held Hell itself in despite,' and, caring naught for the fierce flames surrounding him, seemed bent upon holding a discourse with his fellow-citizen Dante. The great stone lids of these tombs being raised enabled the travellers to see who were placed in them.

From something said to him by Farinata

Dante remarks that it appears as if these lost souls can foretell events :

> E' par che voi veggiate, se ben odo,
>   Dinanzi quel c' il tempo seco adduce,
>   E nel presente tenete altro modo.

To which Farinata replies :

> 'Noi veggiam, come quei c' ha mala luce,
>   Le cose,' disse, ' che ne son lontano ;
>   Cotanto ancor ne splende il sommo Duce :
> Quando s'appressano o son, tutto è vano
>   Nostro intelletto ; e, s'altri non ci apporta,
>   Ńulla sapem di vostro stato umano.'
>
> *Inf.* x, 97–105.

> 'It seems that you can see, if I hear rightly,
>   Beforehand whatsoe'er time brings with it,
>   And in the present have another mode.'
> 'We see, like those who have imperfect sight,
>   The things,' he said, 'that distant are from us ;
>   So much still shines on us the Sovereign Ruler.
> When they draw near, or are, is wholly vain
>   Our intellect, and if none brings it to us,
>   Not anything know we of your human state.'
>
> LONGFELLOW, transl.

The disinclination of Farinata to give information and his covert hints puzzle the poet, but Virgil advises him, while keeping in mind what he hears, to remember that his lady will make all things clear.

> Quando sarai dinanzi al dolce raggio
> Di quella, il cui bell' occhio tutto vede,
> Da lei saprai di tua vita il viaggio.
>
> *Inf.* x, 130.

> 'Let memory preserve what thou hast heard
> Against thyself,' that Sage commanded me,
> 'And now attend here,' and he raised his finger.
> 'When thou shalt be before the radiance sweet
> Of her whose beauteous eyes all things behold,
> From her thou'lt know the journey of thy life.'
>
> LONGFELLOW, transl.

With that he has to be satisfied, although it does not prevent him from constantly asking questions, as one who would be for ever learning.

DANTE'S MASTER

In Canto xv, 27, we come to the pathetic meeting with Ser Brunetto Latini, Dante's maestro or instructor.

Circle VII

This man was somewhat celebrated, being Chancellor of the city of Florence, and learned in science and philosophy.

As a notary, however, he indulged in certain corrupt practices and was obliged to retire to Paris.   Dante had an immense affection for Brunetto and pays a high tribute to his fatherly assistance and kindly teaching.   Into his mouth Dante puts the beautiful lines, 'If thou follow thy star thou canst not fail to reach a glorious haven.'   An injunction to mankind not to fall from the high ideals and aspirations with which they set out in early youth.

Brunetto Latini wrote both in French and Latin, a manuscript of his work ' Le Tresor ' is in the British Museum with a portrait of himself at the commencement.   He lived from about 1220 to 1294, and according to Villani did much in conducting the affairs of the Republic on principles of policy.

Scenery in the Inferno

Notwithstanding the amazing flights of imagination in which Dante indulges, his descriptions of natural scenery are so lifelike and exact that they form an unerring guide as to places

visited during his long wanderings. The districts
of the Casentino and Lunigiana with their braw-
ling or calmly flowing streams often crossed by
him, the views of the Apennines 'off whose
rafters slip the snows,' the marble shoulders of
the Carrara Mountains, the steep ascent between
Lerici and la Turbia (up which a funicular now
takes the lazy traveller), all these and many more
minute details are noted.

The larger rivers of the Po, the Danube with
its beavers, the lordly Rhone, are mentioned, and
even Canto xii, 118, contains an interesting
notice of our little river Thames—'il Tamigi'
where the heart of Henry, nephew of Henry III,
is supposed to be preserved in a casket on a
pillar near London Bridge.

If Dante ever went to Oxford probably he
came to London and may have stood near this
spot looking down upon the river flowing by, and
the remembrance perchance came back to him
years after when writing his wonderful poem.

Hosts of cities are alluded to with their respec-
tive peculiarities: Bologna and her leaning towers,
the Venice Arsenal, Ravenna's pine wood, Naples,

Brindisi, Assisi, Siena, &c., &c., and distant
Avignon and Paris.

The reference to blinding mists amongst the
Alps 'like the membrane over the eyes of a
mole' tells us of his journeys amongst the great
northern barriers of Italy; whilst the description
of the Lake of Garda, Benaco of the ancients,
has immortalised that beautiful spot in these
lines—

Circle   Suso in Italia bella giace un laco
VIII   A piè dell' Alpe, che serra Lamagna
             Sovra Tiralli, c' ha nome Benaco.
          Per mille fonti, credo, e più si bagna,
             Tra Garda e Val Camonica, Apennino,
             Dell' acqua che nel detto lago stagna.
          Luogo è nel mezzo là, dove il trentino
             Pastore, e quel di Brescia, e il Veronese
             Segnar potrìa, se fesse quel cammino.
          Siede Peschierà, bello e forte arnese
             Da fronteggiar Bresciani e Bergamaschi,
             Ove la riva intorno più discese.
          Ivi convien che tutto quanto caschi
             Ciò che'n grembo a Benaco star non può,
             E fassi fiume giù pei verdi paschi.
          Tosto che l'acqua a correr mette co',
             Non più Benaco, ma Mincio si chiama
             Fino a Governo, dove cade in Po.

Inf. xx, 61.

A lake there lies, at foot of that proud Alp
That o'er the Tyrol locks Germania in,
Its name Benacus, from whose ample breast
A thousand springs, methinks, and more, between
Camonica and Garda, issuing forth,
Water the Apennine.   There is a spot
At midway of that lake, where he who bears
Of Trento's flock the pastoral staff, with him
Of Brescia, and the-Veronese, might each
Passing that way his benediction give.
A garrison of goodly site and strong
Peschiera stands, to awe with front opposed
The Bergamese and Brescian, whence the shore's
More slope each way descends.   There, whatsoe'er
Benacus' bosom holds not, tumbling o'er
Down falls, and winds a river flood beneath
Through the green pastures.   Soon as in his course
The stream makes head, Benacus then no more
They call the name, but Mincius, till at last
Reaching Governo, into Po he falls.

                                        CARY, transl.

Landino refers, in commenting on this passage,
to the ancient myth as to the bottom of the Lago
di Garda being covered with dust of gold, on
which fed a certain kind of carp only to be found
in these waters.   It is not surprising that some
writers point out the tumbled region of uncouth
and cavernous rocks near the north of this lake
as the spot which suggested the landscape in the

F

Inferno; other authorities give the neighbourhood of Naples as the chosen place, whilst others
again point to the ancient fortified city of Les
Baux in Provence. Dante certainly went there
when at Avignon, so not without a show of reason
are the enormous serrated rocks forming a natural
amphitheatre pointed out as the entrance to the
Infernal Circles, especially as Dante appears to
have Italianised the Provençal word 'baus' into
balzo, which he uses to denote the escarpments
or shelves of rock.

THE ANCIENT IMAGE AT LUCCA

Circle
VIII

Although many beautiful passages occur in
these strange pages they cannot all be pointed
out, nor can the journey be followed step by step,
but it is well to note that an illuminating ray
of light is thrown across the dark pages of
Canto xxi by the mention of 'Il Volto Santo'
—that sacred Face or Image of Christ which still
exists and is preserved with veneration in the
Cathedral of Lucca. The multitude of those
being tormented in the 5th Bolgia of the 8th

Circle for the sin of peculation, or bartering of offices (i barattieri), seems to consist principally of the Lucchese, for Dante points out one of the 'Anziani' of Santa Zita, and goes on to declare—

> A quella terra che n'è ben fornita:
> Ogn' uom v'è barattier, fuor che Bonturo.

> Behold one of the elders of Saint Zita;
> Plunge him beneath, for I return for others
> Unto that town, which is well furnished with them,
> All there are barrators, except Bonturo.

These last three words are ironical and have been turned into a proverb, since Bonturo Dati was a renowned peculator, and trafficker in offices of state to his own private advantage, and Pope Boniface is reported to have said of him, 'Tu diguazzo mezzo Lucca' (Thou dost spoil the half of Lucca).

On the bridge overlooking the terrible depths below stand the Demons crying out to the wretched sinners, 'Here is no place for the Sacred Face,' and well would the inhabitants of Lucca understand the sarcasm underlying that remark, as they were all accustomed for centuries to call upon 'il Volto Santo' (the Sacred Face) when they needed assistance.

The story of this very ancient and rudely carved image, supposed to be the real likeness of the Christ, is a strange one. Landino in his commentary relates the following tale which he drew from the chronicles of Benvenuto da Imola :

'Nicodemus, the disciple of Christ, made a likeness of the natural face of Christ, which when he died he left to Issachar; this man for fear of the Jews kept it hidden; in succession it passed to his descendants.

'Finally it fell into the hands of one Salentio, a Christian living in Jerusalem.

'There came at that time to visit the Holy Sepulchre a holy Bishop called Gualfredo, and by a revelation he saw it in a dream, and it was revealed to him where this "Santo Volto" was to be found.

'With much ingenuity and many prayers he obtained it from Salentio, and carried it to the city of Joppa, and here through Divine Grace a much ornamented vessel appeared, which moving without the help of sails or oars conducted it to

the port of Luni.   The Lucchese were stupefied
with wonder by this miracle, and wishing to enter
the ship they found they could not touch it until
the arrival of the Bishop of Lucca, Giovanni by
name.'

Much discussion arose as to the eventual
destination of the precious relic, since both the
port of Luni and the city of Lucca claimed it.
The matter was decided by the Bishop, who
ordered some white oxen, which had never drawn
a burden, to be harnessed to a new cart and the
sacred image to be placed upon it.   This being
done the oxen were allowed to go which way
they pleased.   With no hesitation they instantly
started for Lucca, and carried the precious relic
to the Church of S. Martino, where with great
veneration it was deposited more than 1000 years
ago, and there it remains to this present day, an
image evidently of most ancient workmanship.

DANTE AND THE GREEK LANGUAGE

The interesting question as to whether Dante
did or did not understand Greek comes up when

Canto xxvi is reached, for here he meets Ulysses and Diomed 'running together in punishment,' and earnestly entreats that he may be allowed to speak with them. Virgil prefers to address them instead, because the shades being Greeks might despise Dante's words. But Dante describes himself as *hearing and understanding* the words spoken to them by Virgil, and the voice which replied (line 90) certainly seems to have used a language understood by Dante.

The whole description of the last voyage of Ulysses may be imaginary, but it is very interesting, with its details of crossing the Equator, and the view of the high mountain, dim in the distance, which some commentators take for the mount of Purgatory, others for one of the mountains of Morocco.

If we turn back to Canto v of the *Inferno* it may be well to remember that the words 'Nessun maggior dolore' are supposed to be a quotation from the Greek of Aeschylus, and there is an allusion to '*i mysterii*' in the *Vita Nuova* which is from the Greek; this rather goes to prove that Dante did know a little Greek. Although

translations had made him familiar with the
works of some ancient Greek writers, Homer's
works had not yet been done into Latin, as
Dante tells us in the *Convito* 1, 7, 51. 'Nothing
which is harmonised by the rhythmic chain can
be translated from its own tongue into another
without breaking all its sweetness and harmony.
This is the reason why Homer has not been
translated from Greek into Latin like the other
writings of the Greeks which we have.'

A copy of the Iliad which belonged to Guido
Novello da Polenta, who befriended Dante during
the last years of his life, found its way to the
Ambrosian Library at Milan. One can well
believe that many were the conversations held
by Dante and his poetic patron over this old
manuscript, should it really have been his.

DANTE'S RELATIONS WITH VIRGIL

A delightful human touch is to be noticed at
the end of Canto xxx and the beginning of
Canto xxxi when Virgil, finding his follower's
curiosity had got the better of good taste, and

was leading him to linger too long listening to some sad laments, pours forth the bitter words: 'Che vuol cio udire e bassa voglia' (He who wishes to hear *that* is base of will) and brings the flaming colour to Dante's cheeks. Then the sweet Guide, feeling perhaps sorry to have had to give such a reproof, commences by kind words to reassure him. Thus may a true friend caution another by a needful rebuke if he hastens at the same time to show his feeling of affection. Dante with thankfulness exclaims:

> Una medesma lingua pria mi morse,
>   Sì che mi tinse l'una e l'altra guancia,
>   E poi la medicina mi riporse.
>
> *Inf.* xxxi, 1.

> One and the selfsame tongue first wounded me,
>   So that it tinged the one cheek and the other,
>   And then held out to me the medicine.
>
> LONGFELLOW, transl.

The thoughtful kindness with which the great Latin poet is described as guiding Dante's footsteps, and instructing him in all needful knowledge, is one of the most striking things depicted in this poem. Virgil is credited with never forgetting how Dante carries with him his human body, together with all the darkness and bewilderment of a mind not open yet to receive perfect knowledge. It seems sad, so very sad, the fact of this lofty gracious soul being relegated to Limbo, and yet being permitted to travel even through the Purgatorio up to Terrestrial Paradiso without the hope of remaining there, coming almost to the Heavenly Paradiso, and then turning back with the vacant look of wonder on his face, when Dante at last meets his Beatrice standing on the edge of the triumphal car of the Church.

Perhaps Dante judges that he is happier in the dim light amongst the company of other great poets pacing the quiet fields with no restless longing or green leaf of hope. But one wishes the great Florentine had expressed some desire that Virgil should attain to the supreme vision of God. There seems to be no passage indicating such a wish, and of course from the allegorical and symbolical point of view human wisdom cannot pierce to the heavenly mysteries, but must retire before Divine Wisdom which is the only infallible guide.

To quote the words of a far-seeing modern lecturer on this point. 'Dante feared lest his own intellect should lead him to forsake the orthodox faith, or to an undue love of science which would divert him from that contemplation which alone enables man to apprehend God. The intellect which by its own unaided efforts sought to know the unknowable was in Dante's view sinful, and could not succeed.' This is no doubt the attitude he took up with regard to Virgil when using him as a type of human wisdom. The Latin poet Statius, who lived about seventy years after Virgil's time (having been born in Naples during the 6th decade after Christ), on meeting the travellers in *Purgatorio* is described as wishing to worship Virgil, giving him high praise, and making use of these remarkable words :

> Thou first directedst me
> Towards Parnassus, in its grots to drink,
> And first concerning God didst me enlighten.
> Thou didst as he who walketh in the night,
> Who bears his light behind, which helps him not,
> But wary makes the persons after him.

When thou didst say : 'The age renews itself,
  Justice returns, and Man's primeval time,
  And a new progeny descends from heaven.'
Through thee I Poet was, through thee a Christian.
            Pur. xxii, 64: LONGFELLOW, transl.

Honours were showered upon Virgil by the
Emperor Augustus, and it is clear that Dante
recognised not only the scientific and literary
character of his predecessor in the art of poetry,
but also knew him for a man of upright and
noble mind leading forward men's minds to the
source of all Good in a dark age before the
coming of Christ.

The Latin words which embody the supposed
prophecy of the coming of Christ, and caused
Virgil to be regarded as one of the precursors
of religious truth in the midst of the Pagan
world, are to be found in the 4th Eclogue,
lines 5–9 :

Magnus ab integro sæclorum nascitur ordo.
Jam redit et Virgo, redeunt Saturnia regna :
Jam nova progenies cœlo demittitur alto.
Tu modo nascenti puero, quo ferrea primum
Desinet, ac toto surget gens aurea mundo.

The last great age, foretold by sacred rhymes,
Renews its finish'd course : Saturnian times

Roll round again ; and mighty years, begun
From their first orb, in radiant circles run.
The base degen'rate iron offspring ends ;
A golden progeny from Heav'n descends.

In giving this translation Dryden reminds us
that many of the verses in the 4th Eclogue
are translated by Virgil from the writings of one
of the Sybils who prophesied of our Saviour's
birth, and the words referred to are quoted by
Statius as a reason for his embracing Christianity.
The Sybils are supposed to have had access to
Jewish writings and Hebrew traditions, and this
accounts for the prophecies which embody the
idea of a coming Saviour of mankind. It is
remarkable how wide a place the Sybils take in
decorative art, they are constantly depicted in
frescoes and paintings.

On the wonderful graffito pavement in the
Duomo at Siena the Cuman Sybil is represented
holding in one hand the golden bough, which
Æneas had to fetch from the dark shades before
she led him down into the nether world, and
in the other hand she holds a scroll bearing
the quotation given above.

It is well said that when a man is twenty
steps in advance of his own time, everyone will
follow and praise him as the guide, and when
he is more than a thousand steps ahead of his
generation he becomes invisible, and long after
the world walks in his footsteps. This seems
specially applicable to Virgil. He was a mathe-
matician and astrologer as well as a philosopher,
and Dante thus extols his beautiful poetic style :
' art thou that fountain which spreads abroad so
wide a river of speech ? '

Further down the ages at the request of the
Mantuans our own Tennyson penned some
beautiful and appreciative lines on the 19th
centenary of the birth of the Swan of Mantua,
saluting him as ' Wielder of the stateliest measure
ever moulded by the lips of man.'

The great Italian poet of 1300 A.D. did not,
however, follow his Latin forerunner of the last
century before Christ in making use of this stately
measure, for he wrote the *Divina Commedia* in
' the humble speech of ordinary life in which
even women converse ' ! He ' gave a voice to
Italy,' and wherever Italian is spoken there the

beauties of this poem can be recognised and enjoyed without any classical study, which accounts for its widespread popularity, and the fact that in many parts of Italy the lines are quoted even by peasants. To understand the varied interpretations is a different thing, and in order to attain to this end Chairs were founded in various schools in Italy where the poem was expounded like a classic, which it has now become.

THE TOWER OF FAMINE

CIRCLE
IX
CAINA

In returning now to the journey through the *Inferno* notice must be taken of the terrible but magnificent opening to Canto xxxiii which is perhaps the most famous passage in all the *Divina Commedia*, and especially lends itself for declamation by those of Dante's compatriots who well understand the art. Fixed firmly in the ice two desperate traitors to their country, Count Ugolino and the Archbishop Ruggiero, are yet able to move so as to prey upon and torment each other as they had done in earthly life. Ruggiero is silent while Ugolino raises his head

and tells in bitter and touching words the account
of his imprisonment and death in the tower of
famine with sons and grandsons, Gaddo and
Uguccione, il Brigate, Arrigo and Anselmuccio.

The story briefly is that Ugolino, a Pisan noble
and a Guelph, had joined with the Archbishop
Ruggiero against Nini di Gallura, a nephew of
the Count, and had driven him out of Pisa.   The
Archbishop, growing jealous of Ugolino's power,
brought charges against him of having sold
fortresses belonging to the Pisans to the enemy,
and managed to get Ugolino shut up in a tower,
called for evermore 'the Tower of Famine.'
There after some weeks of imprisonment the
luckless Count and his children were left to their
fate, and deprived of food they died one after the
other.   No translation will be given of such a
passage, it should be read in Italian.   The tale of
the evil dream followed by the awakening to see
terror depicted in each other's faces, the imploring cry from the children for bread, the description of the last locking of the tower door is truly
graphic, and the bitter remark which Ugolino
throws to the listening Poet is soul-stirring:

Ben se' crudel, se tu già non ti duoli,
   Pensando ciò ch' al mio cor s' annunziava :
E se non piangi, di che pianger suoli?
                              Inf. xxxiii, 40.

Cruel indeed art thou, if yet thou grieve not,
   Thinking of what my heart foreboded me,
And weep'st thou not, what art thou wont to weep at?
                              LONGFELLOW, transl.

Truly it is enough to make one weep to hear the caressing words of the little ' Anselmuccio Mio ' :

Tu guardi sì, padre, che hai?

They wept; and darling little Anselm mine
Said : ' Thou dost gaze so, father, what doth ail thee?'
                              LONGFELLOW, transl.

and to mark the struggle of the unfortunate man to hide his feelings and the devotion with which the younger men threw themselves at his feet :

Ahi dura terra, perchè non t'apristi?

Ah! obdurate earth, wherefore didst thou not open?

was his frantic cry before the terrible gradual ending day by day of the young lives, until at last he himself, blind and desperate, groped over their loved bodies before death mercifully released him.

Dante burst forth into words of scorn against
Pisa where such horrors were perpetrated :

> Ahi ! Pisa, vituperio delle genti
>   Del bel paese là, dove il ' *si* ' suona,
>   Poi che i vicini a te punir son lenti,
> Movasi la Capraia e la Gorgona,
>   E faccian siepe ad Arno in sulla foce,
>   Sì ch' egli anneghi in te ogni persona.
> Chè se il Conte Ugolino aveva voce
>   D'aver tradita te delle castella
>   Non dovei tu i figliuo'i porre a tal croce.
>
> *Inf.* xxxiii, 79.

> Ah ! Pisa, thou opprobrium of the people
>   Of the fair land there where the *Si* doth sound,
>   Since slow to punish thee thy neighbours are,
> Let the Capraia and Gorgona move,
>   And make a hedge across the mouth of Arno,
>   That every person in thee it may drown !
> For if Count Ugolino had the fame
>   Of having in thy castles thee betrayed,
>   Thou shouldst not on such cross have put his sons.
>
> LONGFELLOW, transl.

If the Count had done wrong surely the sons
need not have been included in the father's punishment.   The meeting a little further on of traitors
to the city of Genoa makes Dante cry out :

> Ahi, Genovesi, uomini diversi
>   D'ogni costume e pien' d'ogni magagna.
>   Perchè non siete voi del mondo spersi ?

G

Ah, Genoese! ye men at variance
With every virtue, full of every vice!
Wherefore are ye not scattered from the world?
LONGFELLOW, transl.

Verily the turbulent dwellers in the Italian towns were for ever at war one with another, and the perpetual effort for aggrandisement led to many traitorous and evil actions in those bygone days.

THE LOWEST DEPTH

Giudecca   This is drawing close to the Giudecca, or last Circle of Cocytus, the very termination of the bottomless pit where Lucifer himself is placed. Into this fearsome place where the names of only three 'betrayers of Masters and Benefactors' are mentioned, i.e. Brutus, Cassius, and Judas Iscariot, Virgil guides Dante. The bitter wind drives him to take refuge behind his guide, and after one look at the terrible sight which leaves upon the traveller a feeling of being 'neither dead nor alive,' Dante clasps Virgil round the neck. Thus they ascend over the frozen heavy sides of 'il vermo reo che il mondo fora' (the

fell worm who mines the world), until the pant-
ing guide places the trembling Poet on the brim
of the opening in a rock, and on being assured
that they really have reached the other face of
the Giudecca, and that still a difficult piece of
road awaits them he rises up and follows Virgil,
till, through a round hole at the end of a long
rock-bound passage the blessed stars shine forth
to greet the thankful pilgrims 'very early as it
began to dawn towards the first day of the week,'
the morning of the Resurrection.

> Lo Duca ed io per quel cammino ascoso
>   Entrammo a ritornar nel chiaro mondo;
>   E, senza cura aver d'alcun riposo,
> Salimmo su, ei primo ed io secondo,
>   Tanto ch'io vidi delle cose belle
>   Che porta il ciel, per un pertugio tondo;
> E quindi uscimmo a riveder le stelle.
>   *Inf.* xxxiv, 133.

> The Guide and I into that hidden road
>   Now entered, to return to the bright world;
>   And without care of having any rest
> We mounted up, he first and I the second,
>   Till I beheld through a round aperture
>   Some of the beauteous things that Heaven doth bear;
> Thence we came forth to re-behold the stars.
>   LONGFELLOW, transl.

PART III
DEL PURGATORIO

Dante   Beatrice   among the redeemed   A. Orcagna.

Alinari, Florence.

[*To face p. 102.*]

DEL PURGATORIO

Esce di mano a Lui, che la vagheggia
 Prima che sia, a guisa di fanciulla
 Che piangendo e ridendo pargoleggia,
L'anima semplicetta che sa nulla,
 Salvo che, mossa da lieto Fattore,
 Volentier torna a ciò che la trastulla.

Pur. xvi, 85.

Sent forth from the hand of Him, who delights in her before she is created, in the guise of a child who weeps and laughs as in sport, the simple soul who knows nothing save, that moved by a rejoicing Maker, she turns willingly to that which is pleasing to her.

AITH and hope form the pivot on which the whole of the *Purgatorio* revolves, this calm place in which the souls of those who desire to return to 'the God Who rejoices in them' wait and work in hope, until that moment when an intense wish to rise higher proclaims their readiness and fitness for a glorified state.

'A will to move' is the signal, as we see by
lines 55 to 60. *Pur.* xxi.

> Tremaci, quando alcuna anima monda
>   Sentesi sì, che surga o che si muova
>   Per salir su, e tal grido seconda.
>
> .   .   .   .   .
>
> It trembles here, whenever any soul
>   Feels itself pure, so that it soars, or moves
>   To mount aloft, and such a cry attends it.
> Of purity the will alone gives proof,
>   Which, being wholly free to change its convent,
>   Takes by surprise the soul, and helps it fly.
>
> LONGFELLOW, transl.

'It is a noble thing that *Purgatorio*,' says
Carlyle—'Mountain of Purification—an emblem
of the noblest conception of that age. . . . In
repentance is man purified. Repentance is the
grand Christian act. It is beautiful how Dante
works it out. The "Tremolar dell' Onde"—that
trembling of the ocean waves, under the first new
gleam of morning, dawning afar on the wandering two, is a type of an altered mood. Hope
has dawned, never-dying Hope, if in company
still with heavy sorrow, a soft breathing of penitence mounts higher and higher to the Throne of
Mercy itself. "Pray for me" the denizens of that

mount of pain all say to him. They toil pain-
fully up that winding steep bent down like
corbels of a building, some of them crushed
together so for the sin of pride, yet nevertheless
in years, in ages, in æons, they shall have reached
the top which is Heaven's gate, and by mercy
shall be admitted in. The joy too of all, when
one soul has perfected repentance, and got its sin
and misery left behind! I call all this a noble
embodiment of a true noble thought,' continues
Carlyle in *Hero Worship*.

When at last Dante and Virgil issue forth
again 'a riveder le stelle' (to behold again the
stars), they find themselves on the shore at the
foot of the Mount, and with ecstasy at once
remark the

> Dolce color d'oriental zaffiro
>   Che s'accoglieva nel sereno aspetto
>   Dell' aer puro insino al primo giro,
> Agli occhi miei ricominciò diletto,
>   Tosto ch' io usci' fuor dell' aura morta,
>   Che m'avea contristati gli occhi e il petto.
> Lo bel pianeta che ad amar conforta
>   Faceva tutto rider l'oriente,
>   Velando i Pesci ch'erano in sua scorta.
>   *Pur.* i, 13.

Sweet colour of the oriental sapphire,
  That was upgathered in the cloudless aspect
  Of the pure air, as far as the first circle,
Unto mine eyes did recommence delight
  Soon as I issued forth from the dead air,
  Which had with sadness filled mine eyes and breast.
The beauteous planet, that to love incites,
  Was making all the orient to laugh,
  Veiling the Fishes that were in her escort.

LONGFELLOW, transl.

And wandering on through the mists which were rolling away dispersed by the sun, Virgil softly buries both his hands in the dew on the grass, and Dante, turning his stained face to his courteous guide, is washed clean of the dirt from the Infernal regions and regains his usual colour. A reed plucked from that damp oozy bed is girded round him, and thus with the emblem of humility, and his cleansed face, typical of clearing away mists of darkness and ignorance from the mind and letting in the light of religion and wisdom, he follows Virgil along the narrow way.

Antepurgatorio

The travellers move upwards at early dawn, but it will be well not to spend too long in the Antepurgatorio, only pausing here and there to note celebrated people or beautiful passages.

A celestial pilot, like a bird divine, brings a swift vessel to the shore on which Virgil and Dante stand. The boat contains rescued spirits who disembark whilst singing the psalm of thanksgiving 'In exitu Israel de Egitto' as an earnest that the bondage of sin is over. Signing them with the sign of the Cross the Angel quickly returns.

The newcomers marvel that Dante is breathing, and gaze hard at him, 'quasi obbliando d'ire a farsi belle' (as if forgetting to go on to make themselves beautiful). One of them advances to embrace the Poet, but Dante finds on trying to grasp him that his own arms return to him empty.

This shade is 'Casella mio,' a musician and friend who is implored to sing in order to provide consolation for the distress caused by the journey.

The singer begins Dante's own song 'Amor che nella mente mi ragiona' with such sweet tones that even the staid Virgil is entranced, and remains listening to it as well as the negligent spirits. A reproof from Cato, guardian of that spot, makes him ashamed, and he hurries forward with 'haste which mars the dignity of every act' (la fretta che l'onestade ad ogni atto dismaga). (*Pur.* iii, 11.) With a discourse, specially pointing out how 'foolish is he who thinks that our knowledge can pierce the infinite ways,' the time is passed till the steep ascent is reached. At its foot melancholy spirits, like timid sheep, look with awe upon Dante's shadow cast upon the ground, and wonder why the sun does not penetrate his figure even as it does their own intangible ones.

Amongst them, recognised by his golden hair, is Manfred, grandson of the Emperor Henry VI. Excommunicated by the Church and his life cut off suddenly near Benevento, yet was he saved at the last moment because 'infinite goodness has such wide arms that it takes in all who turn to it,' and also because 'by no curse of man is anyone so lost but that eternal love cannot turn him whilst there remains any green leaf of hope alive.' (*Pur.* iii, 133.)

Mr J. Addington Symonds says of this passage : ' It is a noble sentence appealing to God's judgment-seat from that of S. Peter. Dante saw clearly and spoke boldly as his reason and his faith in God's goodness prompted. His catholicity is to be noticed. Humanity was to him one divinely governed family.'

Manfred begs Dante to tell his daughter Constance the truth, so that she may pray for him to obtain a quicker release from Antepurgatorio.

Wearily the poets drag themselves up to the first 'balzo' or terrace where like mountain climbers they sit and rest looking back over their way.

When Virgil was explaining that the ascent would be easier the more they progressed and at the top Dante might expect complete rest, a voice from behind a rock suddenly remarked : ' Perhaps before that you will require to sit' (Forse che di sedere in prima avrai distretta). This proceeded from the lazy Belacqua sitting embracing his knees with his head between them, just as in earthly life he used to lounge at his shop door. Dante, delighted to recognise him, rebukes him for his sloth, as he had probably often done in life. There was only time to receive a request for a prayer before Virgil warns Dante that night is approaching and they must go on.

He presently rebukes him for again listening to the astonished whispers of the spirits at the unwonted sight of a man's shadow cast upon the ground.

> Vien dietro a me, e lascia dir le genti!
> Sta' come torre ferma, che non crolla
> Giammai la cima per soffiar de' venti!
>
> *Pur.* v, 13.

Come after me, and let the people talk! stand firm like a tower which never bends its summit for any breath of wind.

Then appeared a procession of negligent souls 'chanting the Miserere verse by verse' who were also puzzled by the fact that Dante's body allowed no light to pass through. Stopping in their penance they burst into a long hoarse cry of 'O.' The explanation from Virgil as to Dante

being yet alive caused them so to throw off their
negligence as to be likened to shooting stars, or
summer lightning, thus quickly did they 'wheel
round' to pray him to wait and speak with
them. He met with various personages whose
shades are placed here amongst those who put
off repentance till the last moment, such as Buon-
conte di Montefeltro with the vivid description
of his end, and La Pia with her sad history
merely touched in. Belacqua, 'il pigro,' has been
left behind; does he still sit embracing his knees
on that cornice hoping for the prayers of some
righteous soul on earth to help him in to
Purgatorio? Without such prayers he and his
companions must spend as long on the outskirts
as they had spent in impenitence on earth. Dante
is much puzzled as to the use of prayers for
these people, until Virgil assures him that Beatrice
whom he will meet at the top of the mountain,
radiant and happy, will resolve all his doubts.
'She shall be the light between truth and intellect' (che lume fia tra il vero e l'intelletto.
Pur. vi, 45). This gives such a spur to his
desire to ascend that he wastes no more time

in discussing abstruse subjects, but hastens on his way exclaiming that he is no longer tired.

In Canto vi they come to the 'Anima Lombarda' (Lombard soul) who stood proud and disdainful. This is Sordello the famous Troubadour, and of him it is said : 'by the voice of S. Francis himself he had been recognised at a tournay as the bravest of knights.' His reputation is owing very materially to the admiration here expressed for him by Dante, who struck with the noble haughtiness of his aspect compares him to 'a lion in a state of majestic repose'; thus says Sismondi. Roused by the advent of a fellow–Mantuan, Sordello embraces Virgil.

Here Dante bursts forth into fiery indignant wrath against Italy and all the dissensions of that then unhappy and quarrelsome land. 'Ahi serva Italia, di dolore ostello, nave senza nocchiero in gran tempesta' (Oh! servile Italy, hostel of woe, ship without a pilot in a great tempest), and blames the priests who had subverted the Imperial Government. The word 'gente' according to Lombardi being applied to the priests.

One cannot help wondering how Dante would now express himself if he could pen for his countrymen an ode to United Italy. How he would rejoice in finding some of his cherished dreams fulfilled, and Italy taking her place amongst the nations of Europe!

Sordello tells the travellers that they cannot cross a certain line after sunset; this is typical of the impossibility of making progress in grace without light from God. During the hours of twilight and darkness they visit a lovely dell in the bosom of the mountain, where wondrous plants are blooming and strange odours overpower the air. Here are gathered the shades of many kings and rulers who left undone what they ought to have done, such as Henry III of England, Pedro of Aragon, Charles I of Anjou, singing ' Salve Regina,' and beautiful is the description of this quiet spot. (*Pur.* vii, 83.)

Canto viii opens with the well-known lines describing the declining day—

> Era già l'ora che volge il disio
>   Ai naviganti e intenerisce il core,
> Lo dì ch' han detto ai dolci amici addio ;

H

> E che lo novo peregrin d'amore
> Punge, se ode squilla di lontano,
> Che paia il giorno pianger che si muore.

> 'Twas now the hour that turneth back desire
> In those who sail the sea, and melts the heart,
> The day they've said to their sweet friends farewell,
> And the new pilgrim penetrates with love,
> If he doth hear from far away a bell
> That seemeth to deplore the dying day.
>
> LONGFELLOW, transl.

Then one of the souls rises and lifting both hands towards the east, seems to say to God—'None other can calm me'—and there issues forth from his lips the ancient invocation preserved for ages in the Church. 'Te lucis ante terminum'—the Compline hymn, the first verse of which is thus rendered in English:

> Now with the fast departing light,
> Maker of all! we ask of Thee
> Of Thy great mercy thro' the night
> Our Guardian and defence to be.

The rest of the invocation is sweetly and devoutly taken up by all the souls, with eyes fixed upon the circling heavens.

As if in answer to this prayer two shining

angels appear and chase from the valley the serpent gliding insidiously to do mischief. This serpent is taken by Professor Plumptre to mean 'night troubles of the soul when it first turns to God, the black thoughts that assail.' The symbolical explanation of the four bright stars disappearing behind the mountain, and the rising of the three more brilliant ones, may be the ascendancy which the three Theological virtues—Faith, Hope, Charity,—take over the moral ones— Prudence, Justice, Fortitude and Temperance.

After conversing with various spirits Dante falls asleep, and dreams that an eagle with golden wings swoops down, and picking him up in his talons carries him into the region of fire where he is scorched, then drops him at a spot higher up the mount. It was, however, not an eagle but Lucia, spirit of illuminating Grace, who through fire of Love had carried him up to the gate of *Purgatorio*. When he awakes he finds himself alone with Virgil before the three steps of 'goodwill,' those steps which must be mounted before entering upon the circular path of that mountain in ascending which all souls are purified from the sins committed upon earth. The description of this short stair must be given (by permission) in the exquisite translation of J. Addington Symonds:

> Thither we came; and the first mighty stair
>   Was marble white—so polished and so smooth
>   That I stood mirrored there as I appear.
> The second, darker than the darkest blue,
>   Was formed of a rough stone, rugged and dry,
>   Cracked lengthwise and across through all its mass.
> The third, whose bulk completes the topmost stair,
>   Seemed to my gaze of porphyry, that flamed
>   Like blood forth bursting from a smitten vein.
> Thereon God's Angel planting both his feet,
>   Sat firmly stationed on the threshold floor,
>   Which, as I thought, was solid diamond.
>
> *Pur.* ix, 94.

The explanation of the symbolism is well rendered by the same author who says: 'The white and polished marble is purity and sincerity of soul, perfect candour, without which all penitence is vain. The dark slab, dry and rugged, represents a broken and contrite heart: its rift is crosswise, indicating the length and breadth and depth of sorrow for past sin. The sanguine coloured porphyry is love, red as heart's blood, and solid for the soul to stay thereon. Upon the last step, the threshold itself, of adamant, which signifies the sure foundation of the Church, the Angel sits as on a throne.' In his hand he holds the shining sword of Justice. Virgil directs Dante to ask humbly for what he desires, so falling to the ground he strikes his breast three times and craves for the door to be opened. The angelic being smites Dante's forehead with the sword printing seven P's upon it, symbolical of the seven deadly sins to be repented of in passing through Purgatory, and drawing from under his raiment two keys, the one golden which is said to mean the authority of the absolver, and the other silver, the science of the spiritual teacher, he opens the sacred door with the warning that they who look back will be turned out.

The huge and heavy door turned on its hinges to the sweet sound of the ' Te Deum Laudamus,' the words chanted by penitent souls coming to him in waves of sound, now clear, now far away, as though they were accompanied by an organ. Dante did not look back, but following his master up a very steep path reached the first cornice.

Here briefly may be given the names of the sins purged in each circle, and the Beatitudes which are gently murmured as each Angel appears and with his wings fans off one by one the seven P's which had been impressed upon Dante's forehead. As they disappear he becomes each time more free and light to ascend with his human body after the intangible shade of Virgil, his guide, until they reach the summit which is crowned by Terrestrial Paradise, from which point of vantage they can look back down the circles.

PLAN OF THE PURGATORIO

Terrestrial Paradise

Summit

Circles	Sins	Beatitudes	
7th Circle	Carnal Desires	'Beati mundo corde'	Canto xxvii
6th Circle	Gluttony	'Beati qui esuriendo'	Canto xxiv
5th Circle	Avarice	'Beati qui sitiunt'	Canto xxii
4th Circle	Sloth	'Beati qui lugent'	Canto xix
3rd Circle	Anger	'Beati pacifici'	Canto xvii
2nd Circle	Envy	'Beati misericordes'	Canto xv
1st Circle	Pride	'Beati pauperes spiritu'	Canto xii

Three steps at the entrance to Purgatory.   Canto ix.

Antepurgatorio.

The marshy land, out of which the mount rises, produces the rush —emblem of humility.   Canto i.

The circles are here reversed so as to show how the pilgrim journeyed upwards. It is interesting to notice that the Beatitudes are not given in precisely the same order as they are to be found in S. Matthew's Gospel. In the first circle the blessing upon the poor in spirit is whispered forth, and it is followed in the second circle by praise of the merciful, but the 7th Beatitude is murmured in the 3rd Circle, while those are said to be 'blessed who mourn' in the 4th Circle. 'Hunger and thirst after righteousness' are reversed and divided, the latter half of the beatitude only being named amongst the avaricious ones, and while angelic pinions fanned off another P from Dante's forehead the first half of that beatitude was recited in the 6th Circle. Finally in the 7th Circle the journey towards Terrestrial Paradise is concluded with piercing cries of 'Blessed are the pure in heart,' spoken when the last P is about to be removed from Dante's forehead.

THE PENALTY OF PRIDE

The terraces or cornices of *Purgatorio* are described as each forming a circular path, having on one side a descending precipice, on the other the high rocky wall of the mount which narrowed upwards like a cone. The last circle was the smallest, and the flat top was crowned by the delectable country.

Steep ascents led up to these terraces, and on reaching the first one Dante marvels to behold carving on the white marble cornices of the rock at his side, 'so beautifully wrought,' he says, 'that not only Polycletus but Nature would be put to shame.' The Angel of the Annunciation appearing to the Blessed Virgin Mary was so lifelike 'one could have sworn he was saying "Ave."' Elsewhere there was graven on the very marble the cart and oxen drawing the sacred ark. In front a group of people divided into seven choirs seemed to make the evidence of one sense contradict the other, for by their appearance they were singing, but no sound could be heard. Likewise the smoke of the incense there imaged made it doubtful if the sight or smell should be believed.

The description of the rest of the sculptures is wonderful, and reminds travellers of Giotto's work, much of which must have been instigated by the ideas of his friend and contemporary Dante.

These carvings, designed by the great Creator, so absorbed the poet that it was difficult to tear himself away to gaze upon the strange forms now coming towards him along the path. Bent down to earth, under the weight of huge stones upon their shoulders, like corbels supporting ceilings or roofs, those souls who had been overcome by pride on earth here expiate their sin, beating their breasts in penitent sorrow.

In every circle up the Purgatorial Mountain the first instance of every virtue, opposed to its corresponding vice, is drawn from the life of the Blessed Virgin.

Canto xi opens with a most beautiful paraphrase of the Lord's prayer, recited by the humbled shades patiently bearing their heavy burdens. They are addressed by the poet as

'Superbi Christiani, miseri lassi.'   'Proud Christians miserably weary, who with a short-sighted
view of life put their trust in backward steps.'
'Do you not recognise,' continues Dante, 'that
we are worms, born to form the angelical butter-
fly? . . . Since we are thus imperfect insects,
like the grub in which the full form is wanting,
why doth your spirit soar too high?'

Right it seems for these weak ones to call for
help and murmur on :

> O Padre nostro, che ne' cieli stai,
>   Non circonscritto, ma per più amore
>   Che ai primi effetti di lassù tu hai,
> Laudato sia il tuo nome e il tuo valore
>   Da ogni creatura, com' è degno
>   Di render grazie al tuo dolce vapore.
> Vegna vèr noi la pace del tuo regno,
>   Chè noi ad essa non potem da noi,
>   S'ella non vien, con tutto nostro ingegno.
> Come del suo voler gli angeli tuoi
>   Fan sacrificio a te, cantando 'Osanna,'
>   Così facciano gli uomini de' suoi.
> Da' oggi a noi la cotidiana manna,
>   Senza la qual per questo aspro diserto
>   A retro va chi più di gir s'affanna.
> E come noi lo mal ch' avem sofferto,
>   Perdoniamo a ciascuno, e tu perdona
>   Benigno, e non guardar al nostro merto.

Nostra virtù, che di leggier s'adona,
 Non spermentar con l'antico avversaro,
 Ma libera da lui, che sì la sprona.
Quest' ultima preghiera, Signor caro,
 Già non si fa per noi, chè non bisogna,
 Ma per color che dietro a noi restaro.

Our Father, thou who dwellest in the heavens,
 Not circumscribed, but from the greater love
 Thou bearest to the first effects on high,
Praised be thy name and thine omnipotence
 By every creature, as befitting is
 To render thanks to thy sweet effluence.
Come unto us the peace of thy dominion,
 For unto it we cannot of ourselves,
 If it come not, with all our intellect.
Even as thine own Angels of their will
 Make sacrifice to thee, Hosanna singing,
 So may all men make sacrifice of theirs.
Give unto us this day our daily manna,
 Withouten which in this rough wilderness
 Backward goes he who toils most to advance.
And even as we the trespass we have suffered
 Pardon in one another, pardon thou
 Benignly, and regard not our desert.
Our virtue, which is easily o'ercome,
 Put not to proof with the old Adversary,
 But thou from him who spurs it so, deliver.
This last petition verily, dear Lord,
 Not for ourselves is made, who need it not,
 But for their sake who have remained behind us.
                    LONGFELLOW, transl.

When they come to the clause which beseeches freedom from temptation they say 'Dear Lord, this last prayer we make not for ourselves who do not need it, but for those who stay behind.' This pathetic remark causes Dante, the devout Catholic, to point out that if those who have passed over to the other world are always helping us by their prayers, why should not the same be done for them here on earth? It beseems us to remember and assist them constantly with supplication to God, that eternal light and peace may rest upon the souls whose will is being purged, so that 'mondi e lievi possano uscire alle stellate rote' (cleansed and light they can issue forth to the starry spheres).

Dante's minute knowledge of the services of the Church may be noticed at this point. From the magnificent description of the three steps at the entrance to Purgatory all along the journey, ejaculations are taken from the prayers used continually by devout worshippers in the Catholic Church, of which he had been made a member in his own beautiful 'San Giovanni,' the ancient Baptistery that he longed so ardently to see again.

Con altra voce omai, con altro vello
    Ritornerò poeta; ed in sul fonte
    Del mio battesmo prenderò il cappello.

Par. xxv, 7.

With other voice forthwith, with other fleece
    Poet will I return, and at my font
    Baptismal will I take the laurel crown.

LONGFELLOW, transl.

Quotations from the Bible constantly recur in
the *Divina Commedia*, and Dante seems always
listening for verses from the daily Psalms, and
hears the spirits repeat such sentences as 'My
soul cleaveth unto the dust,' 'O Lord, open my
lips, and my mouth shall shew forth thy praise.'

The spirits sweetly sing the *Agnus Dei*, the
Miserere, *Te lucis ante*, *Te Deum laudamus*,
Salve Regina the vesper hymn, *Summæ Deus
clementiæ* the Saturday morning invocation of
the Church, *Benedictus qui venis*, *Gloria in Excelsis Deo;* and all the Beatitudes are recited by
the ministering Angels.

Still passing along the first cornice Dante
stoops down, and peering under a stone carried
by one of these proud ones recognises Oderisi
the famous miniature painter of Agobbio. He,

discoursing at length upon the rising up of artists who eclipse each other, as in the case of Giotto and Cimabue, remarks that

> Non è il mondan romore altro ch'un fiato
>   Di vento, ch'or vien quinci, ed or vien quindi,
>   E muta nome, perchè muta lato.
>
> *Pur.* xi, 100.

> Earthly fame is nothing more than a breath of wind
>   which comes from now here, now there,
>   and changes name because it changes side.

Virgil desires his charge to lift himself up, but at the same time to look down upon the wonderful pavement which was carved with instances of the result of pride and placed beneath the feet of the proud spirits, so that when their shoulders were bent under the burdens their faces should be brought nearer to them.   Here we note again how much the designers of the marvellous graffito pavement in the Duomo at Siena were influenced by Dante's imagination.

The stories of Briareus, Nimrod, Niobe, Arachne, Rehoboam, the fall of Troy and many others are magnificently depicted in *Pur.* xii. This engrossing spectacle has soon to be left, for the Angel of humility appears, robed in white and 'with a face trembling like the morning star.' He guides them up the steep steps between the first and second cornices while angelic voices sing the words 'Blessed are the poor in spirit.' Beating his wings upon Dante's forehead he erases the first P, thus lifting a heavy weight, to the joy of the weary man, and to the amusement of Virgil who watches his efforts to feel with his fingers the rest of the P's still left on his brow.

BLINDED THROUGH ENVY

The terrace now reached is bare and empty. Virgil apostrophises the sun and they go on under his beams for a mile listening to the whispering spirits, not seen but heard, flying towards them, 'parlando alla mensa d'amor cortese inviti' (calling out courteous invitations to the table of love). 'They have no wine' cried one voice, 'I am Orestes' shouted another, whilst a third murmured 'Love those who have done ill to you.' Brunone Bianchi comments 'that since

Circle II

these voices do not come from either the Virgin or Pylades who are certainly not in this place, they are only cited by Angels as recording to these souls examples contrary to envy, which here is purged.   And the solemn example of brotherly love offered by Paganism is to the greater confusion of malicious Christians.'

The 'cords of the whip are drawn from love,' yet a deeply pathetic sight graphically described comes shortly into view.

In the shadow of the rocky wall, clothed in haircloth mantles the colour of stone, sit dreary groups of beings resting their heads on each other's shoulders, listening intently for any sound to break the monotony of their weeping hours.

With eyes which are now sewn up with an iron wire, just as a hawk is tamed, the envious here do penance for allowing their eyes to delight on earth in the misfortune of others, and their minds to desire what was not lawfully their own.   Dante heard them repeating the Litany of the Saints, and on addressing them Sapia, a noble Sienese lady, starts up, raising her chin as do the blind, and she tells him of her foolish acts.   He assures her that he himself will stay but a little while in this circle, but much greater is his fear in regard to the one just passed through. Pride is usually a vice of high minds, envy that of petty ones. Pride, confessedly, was Dante's besetting sin, an instance of it has echoed down the centuries in his own boastful words spoken before going on an Embassy to Rome.

> Who goes if I stay?
> If I go who stays?

But Dante spent long in the purgatory of exile during life, and learnt effectually things which would surely prevent him from having many more rounds to take when he became a shade.

Canto xiv is specially forcible, beginning with the dramatic demands of Guido del Duca for information as to :

> Chi è costui che il nostro monte cerchia,
>   Prima che morte gli abbia dato il. volo,
>   Ed apre gli occhi a sua voglia e coperchia?

> Who is this one that goes about our mountain,
>   Or ever death has given him power of flight,
>   And opes his eyes and shuts them at his will?
>   LONGFELLOW, transl.

I

It is very interesting at this juncture to notice
that after witnessing the penance of the proud,
Dante instinctively adopts a more humble tone
when questioned by Guido and Rinieri di Calboli,
for the answer when asked his name is this :

> Dirvi ch'io sia, saria parlare indarno,
> Chè il nome mio ancor molto non suona.
> *Pur.* xiv, 20.

> To tell you who I am will be to speak in vain,
> For my name makes no great noise as yet.

According to Cary, Brettinoro was a castle
beautifully situated in the Romagna, the hos-
pitable residence of Guido del Duca. Landino
relates that there were several of this family
who, when a stranger arrived amongst them
contended with one another by whom he should
be entertained ; and in order to end this dispute
they set up a pillar with as many rings as there
were fathers of families among them, a ring
being assigned to each, and that according as
a stranger on his arrival hung his horse's bridle
on one or other of these, he became his guest
to whom the ring belonged.

Into the mouth of Guido the Poet puts a fierce

comment upon the dwellers in the valley of the Arno. The hogs of the Casentino, snarling curs of Arezzo, dogs growing to wolves in the accursed ditch round Florence hunting the Pisan foxes, these are a specimen of the epithets poured forth in a torrent with reference to those ever fighting restless neighbours, until the Canto dies away in Virgil's beautiful but warning lament over the wilfulness of men :

> Chiamavi il cielo e'ntorno vi si gira,
>   Mostrandovi le sue bellezze eterne,
>   E l'occhio vostro pure a terra mira ;
> Onde vi batte Chi tutto discerne.
> *Pur.* xiv, 148.

> The heavens call you and circle round you,
>   Showing forth to you their eternal beauties,
>   And your eye ever turns to earth ;
> Therefore He who discerns all things chastises you.

THE WRATHFUL

Smothered in a fog dense and dark as night, the wrathful spirits on the third Cornice rue having given way to passionate anger, and deplore it with prayers for peace and mercy. One of them, a Venetian, Marco Lombardo by name,

Circle III

overhears Dante talking to Virgil as he clings
to his guide in the murky darkness. Marco
addresses him, whereupon a discourse ensues
upon free-will and other subjects. The beautiful
description of the joy taken by God in His crea-
tions is put into the mouth of this spirit, and
begins at the words ' Esce di mano a Lui . . . ';
but having already been quoted it need not be
repeated. (*Pur.* xvi, 85.)

After giving his opinion as to the usurpation
by Rome of the temporal power, Marco retires
with the courteous benediction ' Dio sia con voi,'
and an explanation that the glow which was
breaking with a white ray through the mist
warned him of the approach of the Angel by
whom he must not be seen.

Dimly peering through the clearing mists which
reminded Dante of the skin over the eyes of a
mole, and stumbling on in a world of fantasy in
which he seemed to see examples of wrath set
before him, a far greater light struck his face,
and as he reached the first step of a stair he
felt the stroke of a wing, and heard the words
' Blessed are the peacemakers who are without

evil wrath.' This assured him that the Angel had passed on his way, although the brilliant light veiled his form.

SLOTHFUL AND SELF-INDULGENT SOULS

Night descended suddenly as the poets reached the entrance to the next Cornice where not a sound was to be heard. During the dark hours of rest Virgil beguiles the time by explaining who occupy this terrace, they are the slothful.

Circle
IV

> L'amor del bene, scemo
> Del suo dover, quiritta si ristora ;
> Qui si ribatte il mal tardato remo.
>
> *Pur.* xvii, 85.

. . . The love of good, deficient in its duty, here restores itself; here is plied again the evil-loitering oar.

Virgil goes on to discourse upon love :

> " Nè creator, nè creatura mai,"
> Cominiciò ei, " figliuol, fu senza amore,
> O naturale, o d'animo ; e tu 'l sai.
> Lo naturale è sempre senza errore,
> Ma l'altro puote errar per malo obbietto,
> O per troppo, o per poco di vigore."

.   .   .   .

Amor sementa in voi d'ogni virtute,
E d'ogni operazion che merta pene.

Pur. xvii, 91.

Neither Creator nor creature was ever, commenced he, my son, without love either natural
or of the soul; and that thou knowest.

The natural is always free from error, but the
other can err either through having a bad object,
or from having too much or too little fervour.

.   .   .   .   .   .

Love is the seed in you of every virtue and of
every act which merits punishment.

The love which is guided by a free upright
will enlightened by God, and directed towards
Him and towards virtue, cannot be an occasion
of sin. But when it is turned towards evil or
cares too little for good, or runs too rapidly after
what it takes for good, then love works against
its Maker.

Se lento amore in lui veder vi tira,
O a lui acquistar, questa cornice,
Dopo giusto penter, ve ne martira.

Pur. xvii, 130.

If languid love to look on this attract you,
Or in attaining unto it, this cornice,
After just penitence, torments you for it.

LONGFELLOW, transl.

In the three lower circles, of pride, envy and anger, the love of ill to one's neighbour is repented of; in the fourth circle lack of love is purged. This defect engenders the baneful vice of 'accidia' or sloth, a perpetual hindrance to the love of God and man. It is a habit of caring for nothing, which wraps the soul in gloomy oblivion of good.

The shades in the last three circles will be found to be those in whom love has been centred upon self, or upon unworthy objects. Love has run riot in their pursuit of avarice, gluttony and carnal lusts, for which they are duly penitent.

After listening to Virgil's long discourse which should be carefully studied, Dante muses sleepily upon the information given, but he is suddenly roused by hearing a sound as of a rapidly passing crowd who call out instances both of zealous haste and lazy neglect, and with weeping accents repeat the words :

> Ratto, ratto, che il tempo non si perda
> Per poco amor ! . . . .
> Chè studio di ben far grazia rinverda.

Quick, quick, that time may not be lost through little
love . . . . . for hastening to do good refreshes grace.

Amongst those hurrying shades only one, the
Abbot of San Zeno, pauses to speak to the new
comers, then he follows those others who

cancel, by biting, the sin of lukewarmness.

Dante, wearied with the long discourse, drops
into sleep, and is visited by strange and disturbing dreams.

The Avaricious and the Prodigal

Circle
V

Journeying sadly along next morning when the
sun rode high, the poets met the Angel of the
cornice with outstretched swan-like wings, who
in beauteous tones directed them, and fanned off
another P. from Dante's forehead, murmuring
the words ' Blessed are they that mourn for they
shall be comforted.'

Virgil exhorts his pupil, who still gazed earth-
wards, to forget his dream and free himself from
vice, 'to spurn earth with his heels and raise his
eyes to where the eternal King circles with the

rolling spheres.' Lightened and comforted, Dante reaches the flat terrace where they come to the shades who are being purged from the opposite sins of avarice and extravagance. Bound hand and foot these weeping ones lie prone on their faces and the words 'my soul cleaveth to the dust,' come forth with heavy sighs. By day they relate interesting examples of poverty and generosity, but at night examples of avarice and foolish waste of substance are brought forward.

Pope Adrian V and Hugh Capet are prostrate here. The former refuses to allow Dante to kneel in reverence for his office, as he says no earthly position is recognised in *Purgatorio*. Then follows a famous passage in which, notwithstanding the evil which Pope Boniface VIII had done to Dante, he puts into the mouth of Hugh Capet a scathing allusion to the illtreatment received by Boniface from Philip the Fair. (*Pur.* xx, 86.)

The poets had just proceeded on their way when suddenly the Purgatorial mount shook with such an earthquake that Dante turned deadly cold, and then began on all sides such a loud cry that his master drew him close and whispered 'Do not fear while I guide you!'

'Gloria in excelsis Deo' all were saying, and at this splendid sound they stood still, 'like the first shepherds,' until the quaking had ceased and the souls had resumed their occupations. The cause of the glorious hymn being sung is explained later on when a happy soul joins them, and Dante's keen curiosity is set at rest by the information given in Canto xxi, that the mountain shakes to its foundations, and every soul rises to sing rejoicingly with one accord, when any denizens of that land find their will ready to move upward.

While thirsting for information and grieving for the just penance of these shades, a voice behind them offered the salutation 'My brothers, God give you peace.' The voice is that of Statius the Latin poet, and it was for him that the thanksgiving had been offered as he started up from his 500 years' penance for the sin of prodigality as a spendthrift, of which sin Virgil's writings had made him ashamed. (See Canto xxii, 37–45.)

He joins the travellers and gathering from Dante's incautious smile ('ammicca'—literally 'wink') who Virgil is, desires to embrace his feet, but is restrained by the words:

Frate non far, che tu se ombra, ed ombra vedi.

Pur. xxi, 131.

Brother, do it not, for thou art a shade, and a
shade thou seest.

Statius, who may be considered as the type of intellectual culture, discourses very learnedly, gives much information about the holy mount, relates his own history, and also enquires the fate of other Latin poets. Virgil tells him they are resting in Limbo.

He travels on with Virgil and Dante, and enters the river Eunoë when the latter is drawn into it by Matelda.

SOULS OVERCOME BY GLUTTONY

The fifth P. having been removed Dante makes an easy ascent, while conversation of interest continues until the way is barred by a tree bearing good and sweet-smelling fruit. It

Circle
VI

grew downwards having its roots above, and a spring of clear water poured from the rock over its leaves. Out of the tree came a voice crying, 'Of this food thou shalt have none,' and also sentences illustrating temperance and ancient frugal habits.

Tearful, silent, and devout the gluttonous shades pass rapidly.

> Ombre che vanno
> Forse di lor dover solvendo il nodo.
> *Pur.* xxiii, 14.

Shades who go perhaps loosening the knot of their debt.

Utterly emaciated, with eyes sunk deep in hollow sockets came Forese Donati, hardly recognised by his old friend Dante who knew not whether to be glad or sorry for his position. Forese explains how people who have given way to excess are sanctified here in hunger and thirst. He praises his wife Nella for her devout life and her prayers for him, but speaks against the Florentine women for their unsuitable dress.

Dr Hogan's comment that ' Dante was as true a Christian as he was a man of refined and dignified ideas regarding social proprieties, and felt that the more women respect themselves the more they are respected,' is well worth noting in regard to this passage.

Various shades are pointed out in this cornice, amongst others Pope Martin IV, who loved the eels of Bolsena and the sweet wine. This company disappeared in haste and soon a second tree came in sight, surrounded by a greedy group who desired, but could not eat, the fruit. The poets, warned not to touch the tree and directed by the Angel of temperance all shining with a brilliant red light, willingly followed his guidance.

> E quale, annunziatrice degli albori,
>   L'aura di maggio muovesi ed olezza,
>   Tutta impregnata dall' erba e da' fiori;
> Tal mi senti' un vento dar per mezza
>   La fronte, e ben senti' muover la piuma,
>   Che fe' sentir d'ambrosïa l'orezza;
> E senti' dir: 'Beati cui alluma
>   Tanto di grazia, che l'amor del gusto
>   Nel petto lor troppo disir non fuma,
> Esurïendo sempre quanto è giusto!'
>
> *Pur.* xxiv, 145.

> And as, the harbinger of early dawn,
>   The air of May doth move and breathe out fragrance
>   Impregnate all with herbage and with flowers,

So did I feel a breeze strike in the midst
  My front, and felt the moving of the plumes
  That breathed around an odour of ambrosia;
And heard it said: 'Blessed are they whom grace
  So much illumines, that the love of taste
  Excites not in their breasts too great desire,
Hungering at all times so far as is just.'

LONGFELLOW, transl.

THE PURIFYING FIRE

Circle
VII

When the seventh and last cornice is reached the travellers are confronted with a fierce fire blown away from the rock and leaving but a narrow passage along which they carefully walk one by one. The words of the *Summae Deus clementiae* fall upon the ear out of the midst of the burning, alternating with ejaculations describing examples of chastity. 'With such food the last wound must be healed.' (*Pur.* xxv, 139.)

Dante perceives many shades inside the fire, they come as near the edge as possible to gaze at him in surprise, seeing he has not a shadowy body like their own.

A crowd of shades hurry past kissing those they meet in rapid fashion, and shouting out instances of the giving way to carnal lusts. The poetical Guido Guinicelli, coming near to his contemporary Dante, discourses in a lengthy way, then points with admiration to Arnaut Daniel, a Provençal poet who had lived in the previous century. They both dart back into the fire which refines them, asking for a word of prayer while they await with joy their moment of release.

Day was declining, and the sun shot forth scorching rays from his red ball when the last Angel of the cornices—the Angel of Chastity — appears on the bank outside the flames singing in a loud voice, ' Blessed are the pure in heart.'

Then he adds :

> Più non si va, se pria non morde,
> Anime sante, il fucco ; entrate in esso,
> Ed al cantar di là non siate sorde !
>
> *Pur.* xxvii, 10.

> No one farther goes, souls sanctified,
> If first the fire bite not ; within it enter,
> And be not deaf unto the song beyond.
>
> LONGFELLOW, transl.

With clasped hands gazing into the fire Dante calls to mind that he is still walking in his human perishable body and remains paralyzed with fear.

Truly the lines in Canto xxvii from 13 to 60
are a magnificent piece of word-painting, bringing
the whole scene in a wonderful way before us.
Here stands the reluctant man clenching his
hands in horror, overcome by a return of that
cowardice which was severely rebuked when first
he started on his journey. The 'sweet guide'
meanwhile, very anxious for the welfare of his
charge, tries with gentle persuasive words to
urge him on.

> Figliuol mio,
> Qui puot 'esser tormento ma non morte.
> Ricordati, ricordati! . . . E se io
> Sovr'esso Gerion ti guidai salvo,
> Che farò or, che son più presso a Dio?
> Credi per certo che, se dentro all' alvo
> Di questa fiamma stessi ben mill' anni,
> Non ti potrebbe far d'un capel calvo;
> E se tu forse credi ch' io t' inganni,
> Fatti vèr lei, e fatti far credenza
> Con le tue mani al lembo de' tuoi panni.
> Pon giù omai, pon giù ogni temenza!
> Volgiti in qua, e vieni oltre sicuro!

> 'My son,
> Here may indeed be torment, but not death.
> Remember thee, remember! and if I
> On Geryon have safely guided thee,
> What shall I do now I am nearer God?

Believe for certain, shouldst thou stand a full
   Millennium in the bosom of this flame,
   It could not make thee bald a single hair.
And if perchance thou think that I deceive thee,
   Draw near to it, and put it to the proof
   With thine own hands upon thy garment's hem.
Now lay aside, now lay aside all fear,
   Turn hitherward, and onward come securely!
                              LONGFELLOW, transl.

All to no purpose! Dante stands firm, though against his conscience. Somewhat troubled Virgil next tries another bait. 'Now look, my son, between Beatrice and thee is this wall.'

The magic name of Beatrice works the charm, and with Virgil leading the way Dante eagerly passes through the wall of fire in the hope of beholding her. The intense heat is described as making him desire to fling himself into molten glass, but Virgil gives encouragement and declares that:

Gli occhi suoi già verder parmi.
                    Pur. xxvii, 54.

I seem already to behold her eyes.

Guided by an angelic voice they issued from the fire. '*Venite benedicti Patris mei*'! rang forth out of a great light in front. Admonished

K

to hasten on they breasted but a few steps of the
ascent before the rays of the sun departed, then
they sank down each making of a step a bed, and
slumber overtook them on this the last night in
Purgatorio.

Towards dawn, in that hour when Venus is
most bright, a dream came to Dante which
shadowed forth his doings of the next day, and
to the meaning of this dream Ruskin in *Modern
Painters* gives us a clue. ' Leah and Rachel are
the types of unglorified active and contemplative
powers of man : Leah gathers flowers for herself,
and delights in her own labour, and Rachel sits
looking at herself and delights in her own image
—but Matelda and Beatrice whom Dante meets
next day are the types of the same powers glorified. Matelda rejoices in God's labour, and
Beatrice in the sight of God's face. Dante dis-
tinguishes in both cases not between earth and
heaven, but between perfect and imperfect
happiness.'

> E già, per gli splendori antelucani,
> Che tanto ai peregrin surgon più grati,
> Quanto tornando albergan men lontani,

Le tenebre fuggian da tutti i lati,
  E il sonno mio con esse ; ond' io leva' mi,
  Veggendo i gran maestri già levati.

Pur. xxvii, 109.

And now before the antelucan splendours
  That unto pilgrims the more grateful rise,
  As, home-returning, less remote they lodge,
The darkness fled away on every side,
  And slumber with it ; whereupon I rose,
  Seeing already the great Masters risen.

LONGFELLOW, transl.

The splendours of the dawn had arrived, darkness was fleeing on all sides and his sleep with it when Dante woke to find his companions already arisen. Virgil tells him that 'quel dolce pome' —the sweet fruit of Divine knowledge, the cure for all mortal sorrow—will on this day still his hunger ; the prospect fills him with such delight that he feels his wings growing at every step. When they had reached Terrestrial Paradise Virgil fixed his eyes upon Dante and said, ' The temporal and eternal fire hast thou seen, my son, and thou art come to a place where I can discern no longer. I have brought thee here through the use of art and genius, thine own pleasure take now for guide, having issued forth from the steep and narrow ways. See there the sun which shines upon thy forehead, see the herbs, flowers, and bushes which this land alone can produce. Whilst thou dost await those beautiful rejoicing eyes, which with weeping made me come to thee, sit down thou canst, or go towards her. Expect no more any word from me, nor my signal; free, upright, whole is thy judgment, and a fault it would be not to follow its guidance, therefore I crown and mitre thee over thyself.'

In these significant words Virgil tries to explain to Dante that he is leaving him, but our wandering poet is so filled with anticipation that he takes but little heed, and instantly becomes 'vago già di cercar dentro e dintorno la divina foresta spessa e viva' (eager already to search in and around the heavenly forest of dense and living green).

TERRESTRIAL PARADISE

The forest is very beautiful and the sweet smell, the light wind which gently fans his forehead, the murmuring of the birds in the trees above the clear yet dark and shaded stream flowing through this enchanted land, a remembrance of his beloved pinewood at Ravenna, engross all his thoughts, his curiosity being further heightened by the sight of a lovely lady gathering flowers on the further bank of the stream.

With eager words he addresses her, and she then explains many things, admitting him to the mysteries of the rise of that wonderful river, the love of the Creator in giving mankind such a blissful spot and their folly in so soon having to leave it.

> Lo sommo Bene, che solo a sè piace,
>   Fece l'uom buono, e il ben di questo loco
>   Diede per arra a lui d'eterna pace.
>   *Pur.* xxviii, 91.

> The Good Supreme, sole in itself delighting,
>   Created man good, and this goodly place
>   Gave him as hansel of eternal peace.
>   LONGFELLOW, transl.

Landino explains the allegory of the terrestrial Paradise thus: the active life of the purified Christian soul while a citizen of Jerusalem below, that it may at length rise to the contemplation of the Heavenly Jerusalem. The 'oliva'—the sweet savour arising from the flowers or active works of the purified soul.

The 'aura dolce' (sweet air)—the Holy Spirit coming from the east, representing God—bends the leaves westward, that is the active life concerned in administering rightly the things of this world. Yet the leaves are not so bent down as to disturb the songs of the birds, the heart of man is not so engrossed with worldly things as to forget the praise of God.

The stream with its tiny waves which move brown, brown . . . (rio con sue picciole onde che muova bruna bruna . . .) means that the life of these purified ones flows under perpetual shade, free from the sun of prosperity, or moon of adversity.

Continuing her speech Matelda tells Dante that the river is divided into two forks, one being called Lethe which has the property of removing from the mind all memory of sin, the other Eunoë whose healing properties restore the memory of good and joyous things. The reference made by this lady to the Classic poets (Canto xxviii, 145) causes Dante to turn and look at his companions Virgil and Statius, and by the smile upon their countenances he sees that they understand and are amused at her remarks about Parnassus.

Listening to her soft loving words Dante paced along with Matelda beside the stream, when suddenly a mighty splendour shot across the forest, as though it were lightning, and a sweet melody ran through the luminous air. A wondrous pageant passed along the ancient pineta. Dante stood with his left side reflected in the clear water of the river, which likewise carried on its bosom the burning reflection of the seven candles in 'candelabri,' the immensely tall advance guards heading the procession, and when halted the whole was seen by him in the water as in a mirror. He turned full of admiration to the good Virgil, but the sage replied with a heavy weight of wonder on his face not less intense than that on Dante's own. This is the last moment of the journey together of the two poets, although Dante did not know it and turned eagerly to look at the lofty things which were

passing. Virgil, type of human wisdom, had not
the necessary theological knowledge to enlighten
Dante regarding the procession of the Grifon,
the Car of the Church, and all the mystic
personages, therefore he retired before Divine
wisdom, typified by Beatrice who is about to
reveal herself.

Landino elaborately explains the symbolic
meaning of this pageant, and he will here be
followed, though many are the explanations given
by other writers on this marvellous canto. The
seven gifts of the Holy Spirit are indicated by
the seven candles, the white-robed company
being the ancient spirits of those who had faith
in 'Christ to come.' The twenty-four old men
in white raiment crowned with lilies are said to
mean the writers of the Old and New Testa-
ments, going hand in hand. The triumphal Car
of the Church attached to the neck of the Grifon,
whose pointed wings reached far up towards
Heaven out of man's sight, was surrounded at
each corner by one of four beasts emblematic of
the Evangelists, each having six wings, and each
covered with eyes. At the right wheel three

nymphs circled in a dance, clothed the one in red, the next in emerald green, the third in white like snow new fallen. These are the Theological virtues, and in the dance either the white robe of Faith, or the crimson of Charity led the way, since the green of Hope cannot exist alone. By the left wheel four other maidens, representing the Cardinal virtues, kept up the dance, clad in regal purple, and led always by the three-eyed Prudence to whom Justice, Temperance, and Fortitude owe allegiance. The Grifon signifies the Person of Christ, represented in His sovereign majesty by the golden head and wings; and in His twofold nature of God and Man, by the blended colours red and white, which like a lion's mane clothed the extremities. The wings signify the Divine Counsels, on the right justice, on the left mercy, and reaching so high they typify that human minds cannot see into the Infinite, another exemplification of Dante's idea that 'Matto è chi spera, che nostra ragione possa trascorrer la infinita via' (foolish is he who hopes that our reason can compass the infinite way). These pointed wings do not break the banded colours, but stretch up in between so as to do no harm by their sharp points—' Si ch' a nulla, fendendo. facea male' (so that he injured none by cleaving it).

After this first group two aged men followed, clad alike and grave in manner, S. Luke as writer of the Acts of the Apostles, he who belonged to the noble calling of the physician Hippocrates; and the other, S. Paul, carrying the sharp and glittering sword without which he is seldom depicted in Catholic Art. Then four of humble appearance, the writers of the other canonical epistles, S. James, S. Peter, S. John, and S. Jude. Finally a solitary old man, asleep, but with an acute visage, he who saw the apocalyptic vision. With roses and red flowers were their heads encircled, so that above the brow they looked all aflame, signifying probably their love shown forth in martyrdom or in fighting for the faith committed to them. Amidst devout cries of ' *Veni sponsa di Libano*,' 'as loudly sung as it might be when at the last day each mortal rises in its new-clad body,' the Car stopped and the multitude turned to it, as to their peace, continuing the song '*Benedictus qui venis*'—and while throwing flowers they repeat Virgil's words from the Æneid, 'O with full hands bring lilies.'

THE REPROACHES OF BEATRICE

This Canto xxx of the *Purgatorio* which we now reach seems to be most intensely human in its treatment, palpitating with life and love, graphically describing the feelings which overwhelmed Dante when he 'felt the traces of the ancient flame.'

Beatrice revealed herself at last to her devoted worshipper clothed in a robe the same colour of goodly crimson which she wore when he first saw her as a child. A green mantle fell from her shoulders, a white veil covered her head encircled with leaves of olive.

Thus under a cloud of flowers which rose and fell from Angel hands around and about, standing on the Car, draped in the three Italian colours appeared his beloved lady, and his spirit trembling within him, by reason of the occult power sent forth from her, he turned with fear to

Virgil. But Virgil was not there, no devoted guide came to his aid; so now when for the one and only time on which Dante's name was uttered, and he felt obliged to answer for himself, he stood stupefied and confounded.

' Dante, because Virgil has departed
do not weep, do not weep yet awhile:
it behoves thee to weep for another sword.'
As an admiral now at stern and prow
comes to look at those who work the other ships
and encourages them to do well,
so upon the left hand of the chariot when I turned at
the sound of my name which here of necessity is registered,
I saw the lady who first appeared veiled under the
angelical garland, direct her eyes to me here across the stream.
Although her veil, which fell from her head
circled with the leaves of Minerva's plant,
left her appearance not manifest, yet
regally with a dignified attitude she
continued, as one who speaks and holds in
reserve the hottest words;—
' Look at me well, I am, in truth I am Beatrice.
How didst thou deign to approach the mountain?
Didst thou not know that here man is happy?'

Pur. xxx, 55.

Frozen with misery he remained listening with downcast eyes to her piercing accusations, until the sweet angelic song of '*In te Domine speravi*' melted the ice which had closed about his heart, and he wept.

Beatrice turns to the Angels and explains how all her efforts during her life, and after her death by good inspirations in dreams to try to keep him in the right way had been useless, so that nothing short of visiting the portals of the dead and craving the help of Virgil would have saved him. Still he could not be permitted to pass Lethe without penitence, and before that is passed she asks him pointedly : 'What thinkest thou? Reply to me, for sad memories have not yet been removed by the water.'

Weeping, Dante bursts forth with a hardly to be understood 'Yes'—and, satisfied with getting no denial, which indeed it was fortunate he did not offer to her, she continues to upbraid him for listening to Sirens, and for allowing vain things to turn him away from following true goodness.

Whether or no Dante means to imply by the use of the word 'pargoletta' (*Pur.* xxxi, 59) that Beatrice here shows a touch of the human failing of jealousy is a moot point with commentators, but it seems impossible to conceive that so high-minded a soul could be swayed, after leaving this earth, by the low vice of jealousy on her own account, though it may be taken to mean she was jealous for Dante's sake of the unworthy objects with which he had allowed his mind and soul to be occupied, those pleasures of youth which should be thrown off when a wise man reaches maturer years, and which still seemed to be entangling this man of middle age. The perusal of the *Convito* inclines one to think that the following of philosophy to the neglect of heavenly wisdom is here intended.

Covered with her veil Beatrice poured her rebukes upon him, yet holding in restraint her hottest words, till at last she told him to raise the eyes which he has kept fixed on the earth with shame, and when he did so he saw her turning to look upon the Grifon. Her beauty surpassed her ancient self, and dazzled by it, Dante fell down conquered and repentant, having remembrance of nothing further until Matelda's voice imploring him to hold on to her, restored him to consciousness. She had drawn him into Lethe up to his neck, and when near the 'beata riva,' whilst the

words '*asperges me*' were sweetly sung, the fair
lady clasped his head in her arms and submerged
him so that he might drink of the stream. Then
the four virtues, in similitude of dancing maidens,
led him before the Grifon and towards Beatrice.

THE PURIFICATION OF DANTE

A cry of 'spare not thy vision' came as a
warning from the maidens when they placed him
before the Emeralds—those clear shining eyes of
the Beata Beatrice whence 'Love had first sent
forth his shafts' — and he gazing enraptured
cries, 'Pensa, lettor, s'io mi maravigliava' (think,
reader, if I did marvel) when he perceived in the
eyes of his lady, the reflection of the image of the
Grifon, that is the image of Christ.

The word 'smeraldi' may be typical of eternal
hope, but at any rate it leads us to believe that
the eyes of Beatrice did incline to emerald, those
lovely dark hazel eyes in which the more green
there is the more sparkling and transparent they
become, it seems to *make* the beauty of some
eyes, and in certain positions with the light
shining into them the effect is much enhanced.

It was thus with reflected light pouring into them that Dante looked into those eyes of which he had never lost the remembrance since he drew them on his tablets in youthful days. Mark this description how beautiful it is. The two do not look into each other's eyes—no—Beatrice turns her gaze upon the Grifon, leading on her faithful one still to understand that it was not to enable him to see her that she visited the region of the dead and implored aid to bring him to Paradise, but that he might through love of her be led to the supreme fount of all Love. The following of Heavenly Wisdom is not *the end* in itself, it is to lead up to the perfect knowledge of the Giver of all wisdom, and the Author of love to man, as seen in the face of our Saviour Christ.

The glorious outburst in the lines of Canto xxxi, 139, is the result of this vision :

> O isplendor di viva luce eterna,
>   Chi pallido si fece sotto l'ombra
>   Sì di Parnaso, o bevve in sua cisterna,
> Che non paresse aver la mente ingombra,
>   Tentando a render te, qual tu paresti
>   Là dove armonizzando il ciel t'adombra,
> Quando nell' aere aperto ti solvesti?

The splendour of living light eternal shone forth in such a marvellous way when Beatrice stood unveiled under the arch of the heavens which move in eternal harmony, that would not even the palest student, and he who had drunk most deeply of the Parnassian spring, yet feel his mind encumbered when endeavouring to express in words this glorious apparition? For a short while Dante's eyes were bent upon satisfying his ten years' thirst, the ten years spent in sorrow and perhaps sin, after the loss of his beloved lady, until at last recalled by the words 'troppo fisso' (too fixedly) he found himself blinded and unable to see other objects.

Cantos xxx and xxxi should be carefully studied, the poetical beauties are so many and various. Note the description of Beatrice's appearance like the sun rising shrouded in mists. Canto xxx, 22.

> Ere now have I beheld, as day began,
>   The eastern hemisphere all tinged with rose,
>   And the other heaven with fair serene adorned;
> And the sun's face, uprising, overshadowed
>   So that by tempering influence of vapours
>   For a long interval the eye sustained it;

L

Thus in the bosom of a cloud of flowers
   Which from those hands angelical ascended,
   And downward fell again inside and out,
Over her snow-white veil with olive cinct
   Appeared a lady under a green mantle,
   Vested in colour of living flame.

Then the description of his hard heart melting:

Even as the snow among the living rafters
   Upon the back of Italy congeals,
   Blown on and drifted by Sclavonian winds,
And then, dissolving, trickles through itself
   Whene'er the land that loses shadow breathes,
   So that it seems a fire that melts a taper;
E'en thus was I without a tear or sigh,
   Before the song of those who sing for ever
   After the music of the eternal spheres.
But when I heard in their sweet melodies
   Compassion for me, more than they had said,
   "O wherefore, lady, dost thou thus upbraid him?"
The ice, that was about my heart congealed,
   To air and water changed, and in my anguish
   Through mouth and eyes came gushing from my breast.

The reply of Beatrice to her heavenly maidens
who implore her not to upbraid him is splendid:

Ye keep your watch in the eternal day,
   So that nor night nor sleep can steal from you
   One step the ages make upon their path;

Therefore my answer is with greater care,
   That he may hear me who is weeping yonder,
   So that the sin and dole be of one measure.
Not only by the work of those great wheels,
   That destine every seed unto some end,
   According as the stars are in conjunction,
But by the largess of celestial graces,
   Which have such lofty vapours for their rain
   That near to them our sight approaches not,
Such had this man become in his new life
   Potentially, that every righteous habit
   Would have made admirable proof in him ;
But so much more malignant and more savage
   Becomes the land untilled and with bad seed,
   The more good earthly vigour it possesses.
Some time did I sustain him with my look ;
   Revealing unto him my youthful eyes,
   I led him with me turned in the right way.
As soon as ever of my second age
   I was upon the threshold and changed life,
   Himself from me he took and gave to others.

   .   .   .   .   .

God's lofty fiat would be violated,
   If Lethe should be passed, and if such viands
   Should tasted be, withouten any scot
Of penitence, that gushes forth in tears.
LONGFELLOW, transl.

The final sympathetic appeal of the three
persuasive nymphs is very graceful and these
are the words which they used with glad result :

'Turn, Beatrice, O turn thy holy eyes,'
  Such was their song, 'unto thy faithful one,
  Who has to see thee ta'en so many steps.
In grace do us the grace that thou unveil
  Thy face to him, so that he may discern
  The second beauty which thou dost conceal.'

Pur. xxxi, 134.

Beatrice is stern and unbending until Dante has expressed repentance, then she forgives him, and lavishing all care and loving instructions upon the wanderer guides him with radiant smiles up through the Heavenly spheres.

Canto xxxii opens with the description of the turning of the mystic procession, the tall lights, emblematic of the seven gifts of the Holy Spirit, still leading. After wheeling round 'like a regiment of soldiers' the car is fastened to a tree and Beatrice descends. At the sound of a harmony such as never was heard on our earth Dante falls asleep, it would seem that the waters of Lethe had been too much for him and his acute mind was lulled to rest.

What the symbolic meaning of this sleep is appears difficult to determine. He is awakened by a sudden 'glorious light which rent the veil of

sleep,' and he is bidden to rise, then fright over-
takes him that he has again lost his guiding star.
But she is there seated on the ground guarding
the Chariot, and as Dante approaches the
charmed circle he sees the nymphs in a ring
surrounding her, with those lamps in their hands
which are secure from earthly winds.

Beatrice gives at last the welcome message:

> Qui sarai tu poco tempo silvano,
>   Poi sarai meco, senza fine, cive
>   Di quella Roma onde Cristo è romano.

> Short while shalt thou be here a forester,
>   Then thou shalt be with me for evermore
>   A citizen of that Rome where Christ is Roman.

Yes, after a short sojourn here in earthly flesh
he was to be admitted a citizen of that city of
which Christ is King; first however he was to
fulfil his mission, and write and carry back to
earth what passed before his eyes in the extraordinary vision which was now to be unfolded.
'Therefore, for the benefit of the world, which
does ill, keep thine eyes fixed on the Car, and
when thou returnest to earth, see that thou write
it down.'

Thus Beatrice said and Dante prepared to obey. The succeeding vision typifies probably the evils which befell the Church by reason of heresies, enemies, rapacity of Kings and other disorders which threatened to overwhelm it. Allusion is also supposed to be made to the removal of the Papal See to Avignon.

Upon the rising up of Beatrice to go forward our Poet lags behind, and is admonished for not asking questions. Humbly he answers 'My lady knows my need, and what is best for it.' Beatrice conjures him to throw away all fear and shame, and proceeds to expound the vision to him, but her words fly above his head, so stupefied does he appear. He obstinately refuses to agree to her charge that he has widely departed from her teaching and is thus unable to follow her meaning. Whereat she smiles and reminds him that he tasted Lethe earlier in the day. Presently there opens out before him the sight of the two forks of Lethe and Eunoë, and he beseeches 'the light and glory of the human race' to say 'what water is it which appears from one head and spreads so far and wide?'

Beatrice desires Matelda to take him to Eunoë, the property of whose waters is to bring back all memory of good, and after that sweet drink he returns from 'that holy wave, resuscitated, as new plants renew their leaves.'

Puro e disposto a salire alle stelle.

Pure and disposed to mount unto the stars.

PART IV
DEL PARADISO

Dante and Beatrice ascend to the highest Heaven.
Ancient Italian woodcut.

[*To face p.* 170.

DEL PARADISO

La gloria di Colui che tutto move,
　Per l'universo penetra, e risplende
　In una parte più, e meno altrove.
Nel ciel che più della sua luce prende,
　Fu' io, e vidi cose che ridire
　Nè sa, nè può qual di lassù discende;
Perchè, appressando sè al suo Disire,
　Nostro intelletto si profonda tanto,
　Che retro la memoria non può ire.
Par. i, i.

The glory of Him who moveth everything
　Doth penetrate the universe, and shine
　In one part more and in another less.
Within that heaven which most his light receives
　Was I, and things beheld which to repeat
　Nor knows, nor can, who from above descends;
Because in drawing near to its desire
　Our intellect ingulphs itself so far,
　That after it the memory cannot go.
LONGFELLOW, transl.

ARADISO in Dante's conception means the contentment of the intellect in God, says Brunone Bianchi, a basking in the light of His love.

171

Luce intellettual, piena d'amore ;
  Amor di vero ben, pien di letizia ;
  Letizia, che trascende ogni dolzore.
                          Par. xxx, 40.

Light intellectual replete with love,
  Love of true good replete with ecstasy,
  Ecstasy that transcendeth every sweetness.
                          LONGFELLOW, transl.

Balbi holds that the *Paradiso* must not be considered as pleasant reading for the general reader,
but a special recreation for those who find there,
expressed in sublime verse, contemplations that
have been the subject of their philosophical and
theological studies. But since few will be such
students it seems well to see what Dean Church
says to those who do not study so deeply. ' The
whole *Commedia* is penetrated and is alive with
feeling, with all forms of grief and amazement,
love and admiration, and delight and joy. In
the story of Francesca, in the agony of the
Tower of Famine, in the varied endurance and
unfailing hope of the *Purgatorio*, in the joys and
songs of *Paradiso* we get new and never forgotten glimpses into the abysses and capacities
of the soul of man ; and in reading it you will be

astonished to find moods of feeling which you thought peculiar and unobserved in yourself noted by the poet's all-embracing sympathy.'

The one idea running throughout the *Paradiso* is the eternal and ineffable Love of God, shown forth so that the human intellect may grasp it. The liberty of will with which man is endowed, assisted by the light of God poured forth upon him, enables man to attain to the knowledge of God and in Him find rest, according to Dante's own words : ' Light have ye still to follow evil or good and of the will free power, which, if it stands firm and unwearied in Heaven's first assay, conquers at last, so it be cherish'd well, triumphant over all.' *Pur.* xvi, 75 (Cary, transl.).

Ten heavens, including the Empyrean, there are in Dante's conception of the Paradiso, and many gradations of bliss corresponding to the varying classes of virtue, and degrees of sanctity which the redeemed spirits possess. But none of the blessed ones are envious of the others, as Piccarda tells us when she gleams like a pearl from out of the moon.

Our hearts, whose high affections burn alone
With pleasure from the Holy Spirit conceived,
Admitted to His order, dwell in joy.

Par. iii, 53 (Cary).

Father Sebastian Bowden has ably translated a passage on this subject from Hettinger's German work giving the plan of the *Paradiso*, and so concisely that I have obtained permission to follow it here.   He says :

'The nine Spheres of the blessed, answering to the nine circles of Hell, and the nine stages of Purgatory, are founded upon the Ptolemaic system, with its seven planets, its circle of the fixed stars, and of the crystalline heaven.   These nine concentric spheres form the universe, of which the earth is the fixed centre and irresistible point of attraction.   Composed of two weighty elements, land and water, the earth is immediately surrounded by the two spheres of air and fire, and to the latter all flames soar aloft.   Outside the sphere of fire extends the heaven of the seven planets—the Moon, Mercury and Venus, the Sun, Mars, Jupiter and Saturn.   Each of these planets revolves on its own axis from west to east, and describes a course in epicycles round a fixed invisible point in their Heaven. Beyond Saturn is the heaven of the fixed stars, whose period of revolution is the longest, because farthest from the earth. The outer Circle, or ninth heaven, bears these inner systems along in its rapid course of twenty-four hours, yet without disturbing the individual motion of each planet. This outer circle is the crystalline heaven, or "Primum Mobile," from which proceed all motion, existence, and change. Outside the spheres, above all mutations of time and space, is the Heaven of Light and Fire (of Love), the Empyrean, the dwelling-place of the Eternal Godhead. The Angels and the Blessed, according to their degrees of glory, have each their place in the different spheres, though they are not restricted to them, for in the Empyrean all find beatitude in the immediate vision of God.'

This illuminating description enables us to construct the following plan of Dante's *Paradiso*, following the lines of those given for the *Inferno* and *Purgatorio*.

PLAN OF PARADISO

HEAVENS	THE SUMMIT	
X	Empyrean—or Heaven of pure light. The abiding-place of the Eternal Godhead.	Canto xxx, 39
IX	Primum Mobile, or Crystalline Heaven. Dwelling of Angels—embraces the other Heavens.	Canto xxvii, 109
VIII	Heaven of fixed Stars. Here dwell Saints of special pre-eminence.	Canto xxii, 112
VII	SATURN. Abode of Contemplative Saints.	Canto xxi, 13
VI	JUPITER. Great ones of the earth, Kings and judges.	Canto xviii, 68
V	MARS. Champions of the Faith.	Canto xiv, 85
IV	THE SUN. Great Theologians.	Canto x, 28
III	VENUS. Souls whose spiritual life was marred by faulty human attachments, long since expiated.	Canto viii, 11
II	MERCURY. Souls who, but for earthly ambition would have reached a higher place.	Canto v, 94
I	THE MOON. Souls, who, inculpably, have not kept their vows.	Canto ii, 29

To quote Hettinger again, Dante commences
his ascent from Terrestrial Paradise at 'dawn of
the seventh day, and the sun is rising over the
western hemisphere, when to the left he sees

> Beatrice turn'd, and on the sun
> Gazing, as never eagle fixed his ken.
> *Par.* i, 45.

'Then as he looks upon her, the type of the
divine grace and wisdom through which alone
the soul rises to God, Dante is wrapped in
ecstasy. Outspread on every side, he beholds
a boundless sea of light; his ear catches the
harmony of the spheres, the unison of the divine
scheme of creation, in which no false note sounds.
Beatrice and Dante are, she tells him, no longer
on earth, but ascending with lightning speed. For
as the flame mounts upwards, so the purified soul,
released from its sinful fetters, by the very law of
its nature ascends to God, and rises higher, as it
apprehends more clearly the divine perfections.'

SOULS WHO HAVE NOT KEPT THEIR VOWS

After a rapid upward flight, during which THE
MOON.
Beatrice tries to explain to Dante's bewildered

M

senses why he can rise so fast, the first heaven is reached, namely that of the Moon, which seemed to receive them into itself as into a cloud 'shining, dense, firm and polished.' Shimmering in a beauty so faint that a pearl on a white forehead could hardly be distinguished more clearly, Dante beheld the shadowy faces of the saints looking towards him with desire to converse. And one with eager smiling eyes revealed herself as his playmate of long ago in the old quarter of Florence where they both dwelt. The sweet Piccarda who had been torn from her cloister and forced to marry Rossellino della Tosa by her violent brother Corso Donati, once a friend and afterwards a bitter enemy of the poet.

To Dante's request for knowledge as to whether souls are content, or if they desire further happiness, Piccarda at once declares that

> In la sua volontate è nostra pace:
> Ella è quel mare, al qual tutto si muove
> Ciò ch'ella crea e che natura face.
> *Par.* iii, 85.

In His will is our peace: it is that sea to which everything moves, whatsoever is created by it, and all that nature makes.

To do the will of the Supernal Being is the one absorbing object of the existence of the Redeemed, and then dawns upon the poet this truth :

> Chiaro mi fu allor com' ogni dove
> In cielo è Paradiso, e sì la grazia
> Del sommo Ben d'un modo non vi piove.
>
> *Ibid.*, 88.

> Then it was clear to me how everywhere
> In heaven is Paradise, although the grace
> Of good supreme there rain not in one measure.
>
> LONGFELLOW, transl.

The grace of God is widely diffused throughout the *Paradiso*, although it differs in strength and brilliancy, but in all cases it gives supreme bliss and contentment. Piccarda points out Santa Clara, friend and follower of S. Francis, and the great Constance of Sicily, then singing the 'Ave Maria' she vanishes. Beatrice commences to explain Dante's difficulties by showing him the foolishness of rash vows. Although urgent the necessity for keeping them, unless they are vows which God cannot sanction, she declares that in certain cases the load may be shifted by turning the white and yellow keys spoken of in *Pur.* ix,

118, meaning the authority and science of the Church which may be appealed to in order to loose them.

The whole history of 'l'eterna Margarita' and her shadows, given by Dante, seems so imaginary that it is not easy to guess how much he really knew of the beautiful heavenly body. The ancients were great astronomers, but in Dante's time, which was long before the days of Kepler, Galileo or Newton, the wonderful perfection of telescopes of the present day had not revealed to the astonished eyes of the star-gazers all we may now learn about the surface of the moon. The present theory is that the moon is composed of the same materials as this earth. Thrown off into space as a molten mass at the birth of our solar system, it whirled round in its orbit until the volcanic fires gradually cooled and became at last extinct. Every now and then during the process of cooling the subterranean fires burst up, cracking and scarring the already uneven surface, and forming gigantic volcanic mountains and chains of Alps. Some of these cones have cones inside the centre one and rise to the height of many thousand feet. Thyco is very lofty, and Copernicus 12,000 feet high, while one called Wargentin is like a Stilton cheese filled to over-flowing with volcanic matter which has cooled without breaking down the sides of the cone, as the lava from the others has done. The exquisite shadows thrown across the face of the moon are now generally ascribed to the effect of the sun's rays striking the mountains, thus throwing into strong shade the valleys beneath ; and it is believed by some authorities that the particularly bright streaks radiating from certain of the volcanoes are formed by the pouring over in streams of a peculiar kind of lava which when cooled glistens in the light of the sun ; other observers think they may be due to snow. The dark lines in the valleys are rifts or cañons of enormous width and length. If there be any atmosphere it is so highly attenuated that no human body in the state in which we exist at present could live in the moon. Models are made of the mountains in the moon and then photographed, and thus give a wonderful idea of the impressive scenery to be found there.

While ascending rapidly from the 1st Heaven
—the Moon—to Mercury, that small star constantly hidden from men by reason of its nearness
to the Sun's fervid rays, Beatrice continues her
instructions, pointing out that the warmth of love
from her eyes was increasing because she was
rising to more perfect vision, and she breaks out
into the beautiful lines of Canto v, 19–24.

'The greatest gift, which God of His largess
made at the creation, and which most conforms
to His own goodness, and that which He most
prizes was Free Will, with which all intelligent
creatures were and are endowed.' It is this
freedom of the will which makes for the value
of a vow and should prevent rash ones from
being undertaken.

> Apri la mente a quel ch' io ti paleso,
> E fermalvi entro; chè non fa scienza,
> Senza lo ritenere, avere inteso.

'Open your mind to my words,' says Beatrice,
'and do not forget my explanations (although
not altogether easy of comprehension), since there
is no wisdom in hearing information which you
do not retain.' (*Par.* v, 40.)

Just but Ambitious Souls

The planet they now reached seemed to scin- Mercury.
tillate with keener brightness at their approach.
'As in a pure and tranquil fish pond the fish
draw together round anything coming from outside which stimulates their desire to eat, so did
I see more than a thousand splendours come
towards us and from each I heard the words,
"Here is one who will increase our loves."'
(*Par.* v, 100.)

As every spirit came up they seem fulfilled
with joy.   But one alone, most splendid, began
to address Dante thus :

> O bene nato, a cui veder li troni
>   Del trionfo eternal concede grazia,
>   Prima che la milizia s'abbandoni.
>
> Par. v, 115.

> O thou well-born, unto whom grace concedes
>   To see the thrones of the eternal triumph,
>   Or ever yet the warfare be abandoned.
>
> Longfellow, transl.

This evidently refers to the wonderful grace
granted to the Poet which enabled him to have
a vision of the Church Triumphant before he

had himself left the ranks of the Church Militant. The splendid speaker was Justinian whose earthly ambition had placed him with those who had followed it all too keenly.

Canto vi is entirely filled with the history of the Roman Empire up to the date of the birth of the Redeemer, set forth by the great revisor of the Laws, a task which he says was inspired by God as soon as he had joined the Church. He refers to the Emperor Charlemagne, and finally points out Romeo Villeneuve the indefatigable servant of Raymond Berenger IV of Provence. Then joining all together in a hymn of praise the spirits flashed like rapid sparks out of sight. Dante remained in hesitation of mind, doubting whether to ask for an explanation or not, but Beatrice soon smiled upon him and assured him she would quickly solve his doubts. This Canto vii is one not to be hurriedly read; it should be dwelt upon with all reverence as it deals with subjects far above the understanding of mortal man. Opening with the holy invocation ' Hosannah, Lord God of Sabaoth, lighting up from above the joyous fires of Thy Kingdom,'

sung by the happy spirits, the theme is carried
on by the type of Divine wisdom in the person
of Beatrice, and the great scheme of the Redemption is here set forth.

Beatrice says that because man would not
endure a rein to be put upon his will for his
good, he transgressed the mark, and condemned
himself and all the human race to lie in great
error and sin for many centuries, until it pleased
the Word of God to descend, and by the sole
act of His eternal love united to Himself in
His own Person that nature which had gone
astray. If we look at the Divine Figure on the
Cross 'nulla fu di tanta ingiura,' but if we look
at the *nature* taken by that Holy One then may
we learn that 'nulla giammai si giustamente
morse.' The translation by Longfellow of lines
40–46 seems to explain this passage, and is the
following (the italics are mine):

> Therefore the penalty the Cross held out,
>   If measured by the *nature* thus assumed,
>   None ever yet with *so great justice stung*,
> And none was ever of *so great injustice*,
>   Considering who the Person was that suffered,
>   Within whom such a nature was contracted.

Then another question arose in Dante's mind, namely the how and the why of this Divine mercy, and Beatrice hastens to say at once: ' This decree, brother, is hidden from the eyes of everyone whose wisdom is not illumined with the flame of love, or matured by love. Truly because many aim at this target and few discern it I will tell why such an act was most worthy. Divine Goodness, which spurns from Itself all envy, burns so ardently that it scintillates and displays eternal beauties. . . .

' The Divine Goodness which doth stamp the world was content to proceed through all His ways to lift you up again. For God was more generous in the giving of Himself to make man able to uplift himself, than if He had only of Himself given remission, and all other ways fell short of justice unless the Son of God had humbled Himself to become incarnate.'

To fulfil every desire man is to be reassured that ' his life is breathed into him without stint by the Supreme Beneficence, who maketh him so enamoured of it that forever is it desired and longed for,' and from this, continues Dante, may be drawn the argument in favour of belief in the resurrection of the body.

DANTE'S LOVE FOR MUSIC AND DANCING

Much has been said concerning the love of Dante for music, and his keen perception of the beauties of that art. He notices how one note of music is heard seemingly at rest whilst another floats along (*Par.* viii, 17); he marks the singing of *Hosannah* 'in such wise that he never ceased from wishing to hear it again (*Par.* viii, 29); the music of the spheres (*Par.* vii, 4) when their revolutions are described as 'volgendosi alla nota sua;' the sounds of an organ passing sweet (*Pur.* ix, 144; *Par.* xvii, 44); the gentle strains of the matin bell awakening the sleeping Church (*Par.* x, 139), the *Ave Maria* (*Par.* iii, 121, and *Par.* xxxii, 95), the *Venite* (*Pur.* xxvii, 58), the *Gloria in Excelsis* (*Pur.* xx, 136), besides constant notices of the wondrous music, the song of Gabriel (*Par.* xxiii, 97), the *Regina Cœli* (*Par.* xxiii, 186), *Dio Laudiamo* (*Par.* xxiv, 112), the *Sanctus* (*Par.* xxvi, 67), and again the *Gloria* (*Par.* xxvii, 1).

Music always appealed to him, and he missed the sweet symphony when silence was kept in the Heaven of Saturn (*Par.* xxi, 58). From the singing of the *Te Deum* on entering Purgatory when the heavy hinges of the doors turned at the glorious invocation (*Pur.* ix, 140), on and on through the upward journey song and music greet us, described by one who endlessly rejoiced in harmony and whose ear was trained to understand it. But less stress has been laid upon the fact of his knowledge of the sister art of dancing, indeed the description of the dances performed by the immortal spirits has been somewhat slurred over by those who think it irreverent to depict the saints thus occupied.

Those only who know the entrancing joy of perfect rhythmic dancing; the uplifting of the spirit, coupled with a strong desire to move the foot once more again in the dance when the strains of harmonious music sound, only such fortunate ones care to mark that Dante must have danced in his youth, and have often watched with delight the happy dancers in fair Italia before he described the spirits hastening with loving greeting to rest awhile and speak with him, 'lasciando il giro pria cominciato in gli alti Serafini' (leaving the gyration begun at first in the high Seraphim). The saints like dancers 'resting and ready for the next note of music.' Just such an effect seems to have been produced upon the author of *John Inglesant* when he says ' I have often felt that old dance music has an inexpressible pathos ; as I listen to it I seem to be present at long past festivities. . . . Fancies and figures that live in sound pass before the eyes only when evoked by such melodies, float down the shadowy way, and pass into the future. The explanation of the power of music upon the mind is that many things are elements which are not reckoned on, and that sound is one of them.'

Purified Souls of Lovers

It is after ascending to the heaven of Venus Venus. that Dante meets his friend Charles Martel dancing out of the Circle with the assurance that his love 'would have shown more than mere leaves' had he lived longer upon the earth. He

and our Poet were close friends. This young
Prince of Anjou, titular King of Hungary, who
visited Florence in 1295 with his father Charles II,
King of Naples and Sicily, must not be confounded with the famous Charles Martel, Mayor
of the Palace who governed France A.D. 714. ·

Line 52 of this 8th Canto describes very
curiously the swathing of the soul with heavenly
joy, 'like a silk-worm enclosed in its own cocoon.'

After rapidly indicating the kingdoms which
he governed from Provence on the left bank of
the Rhone, and Hungary, the land watered by
the Danube, to the sulphurous region of Sicily
which would not have him for sovereign, Charles
enters into a disquisition, started by the Poet, as
to the reason for the diversities of human nature,
and winds up with the sapient remark that on
earth ignorance often thrusts those who would
make good soldiers into the religious orders, and
Kings are made of those who should be preachers,
'onde la traccia vostra è fuor di strada' (therefore
your footsteps wander from the road). 'The
mind of God is perfect,' says Dante, 'and He
provides for the perfection of His creatures.' It

is by the mistakes of earthly minds, who look not above for guidance, that so much goes wrong in this world.

In the heaven of Venus Cunizza appears, she is famous as the friend of Sordello the Poet; then Folco the troubadour, who was afterwards Bishop of Toulouse, is pointed out as a shining and dear gem of that heaven whose fame shall remain.

The allusion to 'changing the water that doth bathe Vicenza' is supposed to refer to the act of the Paduans during one of their quarrels in cutting off the course of the river so as to leave their rival city without water.

When the illustrious and repentant Folco shone like 'a fine ruby that the sun doth strike,' Dante thus soliloquizes:

> Through joy effulgence is acquired above,
>   As here a smile; but down below, the shade
>   Outwardly darkens, as the mind is sad.
> 'God seeth all things, and in Him, blest spirit,
>   Thy sight is,' said I, 'so that never Will
>   Of His can possibly from thee be hidden;
> Thy voice, then, that for ever makes the Heavens
>   Glad, with the singing of those holy fires
>   Which of their six wings makes themselves a cowl,

Wherefore does it not satisfy my longings?
Indeed, I would not wait thy questioning
If I in thee were as thou art in me.'
      Par. ix, 70 : LONGFELLOW, transl.

Thus adjured to do as he would be done by
and explain the difficulties, Folco makes a
lengthy reply, and finally 'within a light sparkling as the sun's ray in pure water,' Rahab is
pointed out where she all tranquilly holds the
palm which she gained by placing with both
hands the red cord in the window to guide the
heaven-sent Joshua.

GREAT THEOLOGIANS

THE SUN.   Canto x, one of the most harmoniously beautiful of Cantos, opens with words alluding to the
acts of the ever blessed Trinity at the Creation
of the world, making it possible for every created
thing to be a witness of the Creator, though
manifested in so many different ways, such as
the wonderful system of the heavenly bodies,
the precession of the equinoxes, and other
marvels of nature. It is however solely with—

The greatest of the ministers of nature,
   Who with the power of heaven the world imprints
   And measures with his light the time for us.

namely the Sun itself—that Dante now wishes
to treat, since he has all unaware, through the
assistance of Beatrice, reached the heaven of
the Sun at the moment of the joyous spring time.
Men must believe in and long for its glories, but
they may not be imaged, ' our fantasies are too
low for such a height.'

' Thank, thank the Sun of the Angels,' says
Beatrice, 'that through His grace thou in thy
mortal life hast been raised to a knowledge of
this height.'

Overwhelmed with love to God, Beatrice was
for the moment forgotten, until the splendour of
her laughing eyes caused him to take a wider
vision. He then saw around him a glowing
circling crown of living spirits, with voices even
sweeter than their beauteous vision, and after
a triple revolution these burning suns paused.
Inflamed with love, out stepped the spirit of
S. Thomas Aquinas graciously desirous of ex-
pounding things to Dante, since he has, through

N

the love which glows within him, obtained grace to mount that stairway which 'senza risalir nessun discende' (without reascending none descends).

The sparkling circlet of spirits was composed of Doctors of Divinity and other learned people. S. Thomas points out Albert of Cologne next to himself, then Gratian with his smile, and Peter Lombard.   The 5th light and one most beautiful is Solomon.   Dionysius a pupil of S. Augustine, Boethius, Isidoro, the Ven. Bede, Richard of S. Victor, and Sigier of Brabant who lectured in the 'street of straw' in Paris, make up the charmed circle of twelve.

> Then, as the horologe that calleth us,
>   What time the Bride of God is rising up
>   With matins to her Spouse that he may love her,
> Wherein one part the other draws and urges,
>   Ting ting, resounding with so sweet a note,
>   That swells with love the spirit well disposed.
> Thus I beheld the glorious wheel move round,
>   And render voice to voice, in modulation
>   And sweetness that cannot be comprehended,
> Excepting there where joy is made eternal.
>   *Par.* x, 139 : LONGFELLOW, transl.

The eleventh, twelfth, and thirteenth Cantos,
as well as part of the marvellous fourteenth, are
all devoted to the description of the 4th Heaven,
that of the Sun, and Dante seems suddenly to
look down upon earth and ponder in sorrowful
wonder to see his fellow mortals following their
various occupations, such as 'the law, the work
of the priesthood, or buying and selling, stealing
and toiling, or quarrelling amongst themselves,'
while he is so happily employed and gloriously
received up above.

S. Thomas again comes forward to read
Dante's wishes, and explains how two great
men were raised up to help the Church on earth,
S. Francis and S. Dominic ; the one 'tutto sera-
fico in ardore' (all seraphical in ardour), the other
'per sapienza in terra fue di cherubica luce uno
splendore' (by his wisdom upon earth was a
splendour of light cherubical).

Commenting on the lines 49, 50 in Canto xi :

From out that slope, there where it breaketh most
Its steepness, rose upon the world a sun.

Landino states the word 'Sole' (sun) to refer

to the light which S. Francis of Assisi brought
into the world : ' *Quasi sol oriens mundi.*'

> Però chi d'esso loco fa parole non dica *Ascesi.*
> Che direbbe corto, ma Oriente, se proprio dir vuole.

> Therefore let him who speaketh of that place,
>   Say not Ascesi, for he would say little,
>   But Orient, if he properly would speak.

A most interesting account of S. Francis follows, alluding to his wonderfully holy life, the
tradition of his receipt of the stigmata, and his
humble end. Then follows a panegyric upon
S. Dominic, a worthy colleague.

> Who was a fit
> Companion over the high seas to keep
> The bark of Peter to its proper bearings.

Soon the dance and great high festival both of
song and flashing light to light began again, and
a second circle swept around the first, and songs
which in their sweet sounds outdid anything
known to our Muses accompanied the gyrations.
From out of the heart of one of the new lights
came the voice of Buonaventura, the Franciscan,
singing the praises of S. Dominic.

The lovely little description of his birthplace comes in here.

> Within that region where the sweet west wind
> Rises to open the new leaves, wherewith
> Europe is seen to clothe herself afresh,
> Not far off from the beating of the waves,
> Behind which in his long career the sun
> Sometimes conceals himself from every man,
> Is situate the fortunate Calahorra,
> Under protection of the mighty shield
> In which the Lion subject is and sovereign.
>
> *Par.* xii, 46 : LONGFELLOW, transl.

The town of Calaroga was in Castilian territory, and the royal arms of Castile bear a castle in the 1st and 3rd quarters and a lion in the 2nd and 4th. Thus on one side of the shield the lion is dominated by the castle, and on the other subdues it.

'Domenico' was he called and he became the husbandman of Christ's orchard, a messenger and worker for God trying to inculcate poverty and simplicity amongst men. But his followers fell away from his teaching, even as did those of S. Francis, and more lax rules succeeded the ones first promulgated by the founders of both the Franciscan and Dominican Orders.

Buonaventura of Bagnoregio points out his companions Illuminata and Augustin, two of the 'poor unsandaled men'; Hugo of S. Victoire, Pietro Mangiadore, Pietro Ispano, Nathan the Prophet, S. Chrysostom, Anselm, Donatus Rabanus and the Calabrese Abbot Gioacchino. These complete the second Circle of shining lights, and with this list Canto xii closes.

Entreating his readers to stand firm like a rock that so they may follow the meaning, Dante proceeds to propound most metaphysical statements through the mouth of S. Thomas, who again steps forward to assist him, and since it is needful here to follow the entire thread of his argument no isolated quotations will be pointed out, each reader must study for himself, and having done this will turn the page and reach Canto xiv which by many is considered to be the most sublimely wonderful, as it contains rare beauties of diction, and very little argument enters into the rhythmic lines.

The dazzling brightness, glory, and refreshing peace pervading this part of the heavenly kingdom is brought out especially in three exquisite lines which must have comforted many a sorrowful soul since the words were penned long centuries ago.

> Qual si lamenta perchè qui si moia
> Per viver colassù, non vide quive
> Lo rifrigerio dell' eterna ploia.
>
> *Par.* xiv, 25.

They may thus be paraphrased : 'He who laments that here on earth one must die in order to live up above, does not see here the refreshment of the eternal shower in the Heavenly Kingdom.' If he could imagine it ' death would be looked upon with great desire as the benediction of God' is Brunone Bianchi's remark upon these lines. In Paradise our dim perception of light and love is perfected.

In this Canto also is described the wondrous perfection of the glorified body with which the saints are each to be reclothed at the resurrection. Then there bursts upon Dante the view of new appearances forming a circle outside the other two, and by the words ' O vero sfavillar del Santo Spiro' (O very sparkling of the Holy Breath), it must be conceded that these three circles are intended as an emblem of the Holy Trinity.

So blinding was the light which flashed across space that it affected Dante's eyes, and he could look no further, until reassured by the sight of increased beauty in the face of Beatrice, through which was given to him the knowledge that he had risen higher, even up from the Sun to Mars, glowing with more than its usual ruddy light.

CHAMPIONS OF THE FAITH

MARS   With a heart overflowing with thankfulness Dante describes the appearance of the venerated sign of the Cross rising out of the depths of the planet in a brilliant coruscation, but then his 'skill is conquered by his memory' and he can find no words in which to describe the flashing forth of Christ, but leaves it for his readers 'to see Christ like lightning in that glow' as from point to point, from summit to base moved lights with mighty sparkling where they met in passing each other.

'And as the lute or harp in a harmonious stretch of cords makes a sweet tinkling to those who do not understand the words, so from the light that appeared there was joined together on the cross a melody which rapt me, without understanding the hymn. Well I knew it was of lofty praise, for to me came the words " Arise and Conquer." ' (*Par.* xiv, 125.)

Silence is suddenly imposed by the Divine will upon the warrior souls who inhabit the martial Planet, and being aware of it Dante says:

> How unto just entreaties shall be deaf
>   Those substances, which, to give me desire
>   Of praying them, with one accord grew silent?
> 'Tis well that without end he should lament,
>   Who for the love of thing that doth not last
>   Eternally despoils him of that love !
>   *Ibid.* xv, 7 : LONGFELLOW, transl.

Then rapidly there darted from the left hand point of the Cross to the foot a resplendent star, which coursing along seemed like fire shining through alabaster, and it spake these singular words:

> *O sanguis meus, o superinfusa*
>   *Gratia Dei ! sicut tibi, cui*
>   *Bis unquam cœli janus reclusa ?*
>   *Par.* xv, 26.

O thou, my blood!
O most exceeding grace divine! to whom,
As now to thee, hath twice the heavenly gate
Been e'er unclosed?

CARY, transl.

Turning in amaze to look for guidance in his
Lady's eyes Dante beholds such a burning that
he 'thought he had touched at once the bottom
of his grace and of his Paradise.'   Satisfied with
a sanction to listen and reply, he gives himself
up to a long interview with his great ancestor
Cacciaguida, who, thirsting for this meeting, had
thus accosted his descendant.

The interest which pervades the succeeding
Cantos up to the eighteenth is due to a vivid
description of the appearance in the flaming
planet Mars of this militant soul, who living about
the year 1130 made a name for himself fighting
under the banner of the Emperor Conrad III;
and also to a detailed account of prophetic say-
ings and picturesque allusions to the old life in
Florence, including a long category of family
names well known to Florentines of that date.

'The living Topaz,' as Dante calls him, is en-
treated to disclose his name, and having explained

his relationship (line 94) proceeds to dilate upon the simplicity of the life in Florence in his day, the sober garments worn by the citizens, the home occupations of the women and their quiet amusements, the reposeful life abounding in peace, soberness and chastity; and finally states his name to be Cacciaguida, which he received at the Font in the Baptistery at Florence. Advanced to the honour of Knighthood by the Emperor Conrad, he followed his fortunes in war, probably in the Crusades, and finally 'venni del martiro a questa pace' (and came from martyrdom unto this peace). It would not seem that he could have had much opportunity of rejoicing in the peacefulness described by him as reigning in fair Florence!

Although the Poet must have known his own lineage and ancestry to have been high and ancient, he admits to being much exalted at meeting so notable a kinsman in Paradise, and is aware that Beatrice is not quite satisfied with his boastful outburst, for she stands apart smiling disdainfully. She does not however prevent him from having further conversation, but rather gives encouragement to 'put forth the heat of his desire' since he, like the old mythological Fetonte thirsts for information; 'and,' says Landino, 'surely he is right in doing so, for do not the Scriptures tell us to ask and we shall receive.' Dante conjures Cacciaguida to explain the veiled hints which had come to his ears during the journey with Virgil, and assures him that not only does he feel 'ben tetragono ai colpi di ventura' (well set four-square to the blows of fortune), but 'that an arrow foreseen may smite with less force.'

In clear words the noble ancestor replies that through the Papal enemy Dante would be banished from Florence, he would have to leave everything he loved most dearly, and he would 'prove how salt is the taste of another's bread, and how hard the path to descend and mount the stairs of others.' These passages show with painful vividness the iron which had entered into the poet's soul, and how bitterly he felt his banishment from that beloved Florence for whose good he had worked and striven so faithfully.

But worst of all would be the bad and wicked

company which he must put up with. In these
turbulent days the great lords kept open house
for wandering outlaws, and were kind, generous,
and cultivated patrons of poor literary and artistic
people, thus it is not strange to find that our
poet's first refuge was at the court of the great
Lombard, Bartolomeo della Scala, who became a
true friend to him. There he met the youthful
Can Grande, and of him Cacciaguida is described
as telling 'incredible things which might not be
disclosed.'

Dante then consults his ancestor as to the
advisability of writing his *Commedia*, since it will
not be happy reading for many :

> Down through the world
> Of infinite mourning; and along the mount,
> From whose fair height my lady's eyes did lift me;
> And after, through this heaven, from light to light;
> Have I learnt that, which if I tell again,
> It may with many wofully disrelish.
> And if I am a timid friend to truth,
> I fear my life may perish among those
> To whom these days shall be of ancient date.
>
> *Par.* xvii, 112 : CARY, transl.

'Coruscating' in a flash of light Cacciaguida
replies with no uncertain sound ; laying aside

every lie Dante was to make known his vision, let who will feel its bitterness. To it special honour would be accorded since,

> Questo tuo grido farà come vento,
>   Che le più alte cime più percuote;
>   E ciò non fia d'onor poco argomento.
> *Par.* xvii, 133.

> This cry of thine shall do as doth the wind,
>   Which smiteth most the most exalted summits,
>   And that is no slight argument of honour.
> LONGFELLOW, transl.

It was for this reason that 'only souls known to fame' had been shown to him up in *Paradiso*, or on the Mount, or in the dolorous Valley, for 'the soul of him who hears will not put faith in obscure and unknown examples.'

Pondering over the weight of his heavy responsibility Dante is recalled to his surroundings by Beatrice who conquers him with 'the lightning of a smile,' and although he wishes to continue to gaze upon her she persuades him to listen further to Cacciaguida when he proceeds to point out the celebrated warriors whose flaming spirits shoot from corner to corner of the brilliant Cross in Mars, as their names are called by him.

Joshua, Maccabeus, Charlemagne, Orlando, &c., and then amongst the other lights Caccia-guida spoke again showing his own place,

Qual era trai cantor del cielo artista
(which was that of an artist among the heavenly singers).

Great Kings and Judges

Jupiter—as we call the brilliant planet sur- JUPITER rounded by many moons—that sweet star, the quality and magnitude of whose genius demonstrated that justice on earth had its origin in the 'heaven which they engemmed,' is now reached (*Par.* xviii, 115); and 'the sparkling of love which was therein I saw in that torch of Jove signalled to my eyes in our speech,' says Dante, 'and like birds risen from the river bank rejoicing over their pasture make themselves in a round or lengthy flock, so within the lights sacred creatures flew singing, and shaped themselves into now D now I now L.'

These letters stand for the three first in the Latin lines '*Diligite justitiam qui judicatis terram*' from the Book of Wisdom i, 1,

Love justice, ye who judge the earth.

Other lights descended and formed a lily-shaped crown upon the peak of the final M, singing 'the Good that moveth them unto Himself.'

The remaining spirits after circling round the M formed themselves into the body and wings of an Eagle. Each soul was like a ruby into which the sun's rays burnt and smote therefrom upon Dante's eyes (xix, 4). Marvelling intently, he listened to the combined discourse of those ardent spirits. This 19th Canto is a dissertation upon the justice of God, and Dante comments upon the little power mortal minds have of grasping the meaning and scope of it, no more than has the mortal eye of gauging the depths of the sea.

Therefore should man beware of 'judging a thousand miles away with sight which cannot carry further than a span.' 'As are my notes to thee who dost not understand them, such is eternal justice to you mortals,' sings the Eagle in wheeling round, whilst Dante gazes upwards.

> Unto this kingdom never
> Ascended one who had not faith in Christ,
> Before or since He to the tree was nailed.

But look thou, many crying are, 'Christ, Christ!'
Who at the judgment shall be far less near
To Him than some shall be who knew not Christ.

Par. xix. 106: LONGFELLOW.

The beautiful supplication of Canto xix, 22:
'O perpetual flowers of the eternal gladness,
ye make all your odours seem to me but one,
satisfy, as ye breathe, the great fast which long
hath held me hungering, because on earth I
found no food for it,' seems but half granted as
Dante listens to a long survey of the ill doings
of living rulers, and when the voice of the Eagle
stops all the lights sent forth songs which fell
and slipped from his mind.

He heard as it appeared the murmuring of a
river showing abundance at its source, and like
the sound at the opening of a pipe when the wind
penetrates it came a voice which issued from the
beak of the bird, and desired him to fix his eyes
steadily upon the lights which formed its head, so
that these most important ones forming the eye
and eyebrows should be noted.

David the sweet singer formed the pupil,

o

Trajan, Hezekiah, Constantine, William of Sicily, and Ripheus encircle the eye.

The words 'e meco' (line 55, Canto xx) apply to the standard of the Eagle which Constantine carried to the East.

'Who would believe down in the erring world that the Trojan Ripheus would in this 6th Circle be the 5th of the sacred lights!' is the remark of Dante concerning the last-named spirit.

Ripheus is evidently taken as a forcible example to show the breadth and depth of Divine Judgment. The belief in 'Christ to come,' or in other words the dim glimmering of a Christ-like, God-like spirit shining forth in the actions of some whom we term Pagans, was implanted by God and accepted by Him to their eternal salvation ; and the recognition of this idea by Dante is only one more proof of the Catholicity and wideness of his grasp.

The 'three ladies who stood as baptism for Ripheus more than a thousand years before baptizing' are the three theological virtues, Faith, Hope and Charity.

The peaceful satisfaction which appeared to be

engendered by desiring and longing for the will
of God to be carried out, is so apparent in the
attitude of the saints who form the Eagle that
it brings forth from Dante the exquisite lines,
Canto xx, 73 :

> Like to a Lark, which soars in mid air,
> Singing at first, and then keeps silence, content
> With the last sweet note which sates her,
> Such seemed to me the image of the imprint
> Of the eternal pleasure, by whose will doth
> Everything become the thing it is.

Restless and questioning as usual, Dante urges
his informant to tell him more ; and with a
brilliantly lit up eye the Eagle explains the meaning of Predestination, giving a stern warning that
'Mortals ye should hold yourselves straightly
from judging ; for we, who see God, do not as
yet know the number of the elect.'

CONTEMPLATIVE SAINTS

Beatrice and Dante are now described as SATURN
reaching the 7th splendour, even that of Saturn,
and 'coloured like gold which doth recast the ray,

I (Dante) saw a ladder erected upward so far that my sight might not follow it.'

Splendid lights seemed to pour down, as though Heaven were emptying itself upon one step. Then in line 34 Canto xxi comes the strange simile of likening these brilliant creatures to rooks! At first sight it is most incongruous, but when one notices that the sombre plumage of these heavy dark birds takes on a polished silvery sheen when the sun's rays strike them in the early morn, then the comparison seems less inappropriate. The translation by Longfellow of these lines is as follows:

> And as accordant with their natural custom
> The rooks together at the break of day
> Bestir themselves to warm their feathers cold;
> Then some of them fly off without return,
> Others come back to where they started from,
> And others, wheeling round, still keep at home;
> Such fashion it appeared to me was there
> Within the sparkling that together came,
> As soon as on a certain step it struck,
> And that which nearest unto us remained
> Became so clear, that in my thought I said,
> Well I perceive the love thou showest me.'

The sweet symphony of Paradise kept silence

in this Heaven, even as Beatrice would not smile, because as yet Dante was merely a mortal who could not bear perfection either of sight or sound. Deep love drew S. Peter Damiano down the stair to answer Dante's questions, but when the latter presumed to enquire why *he* had been sent, the spirit waxed very burning in light and whirled himself like to a swift millstone, administering a stern reproof which made Dante feel for once humble. 'Even the Seraph who hath his eye most fixed on God would not give satisfaction to that question, and the mortal world must not presume to move its feet towards so great a goal.' (*Par.* xxi, 92.)

Vanquished by the thunder of a cry deep enough to stupefy the Poet, he turns to Beatrice who soothes him with the assurance :

> Knowest thou not thou art in Heaven,
> And knowest thou not that Heaven is holy all,
> And what is done here cometh from good zeal?
> > *Par.* xxii, 7 : LONGFELLOW, transl.

Great contemplative souls inhabit this planet, a step higher than those active ones previously mentioned. S. Benedict comes forward out of one hundred or more shining pearls and offers explanation as to who are his companions, and points up the golden ladder at the top of which every desire is perfected, matured, and entirely satisfied. Sadly S. Benedict alludes to the degeneracy of the Church, and then rapidly gathering his assembly together he sweeps them upward like a whirlwind.

Beatrice immediately thrusts Dante up after them with a sign, conquering by her power, he says, the nature of man, which is to descend through the force of the laws of gravity.

The Hosts of Christ's Triumph

Heaven of Fixed Stars

The spot now reached is supposed to be Dante's natal sign of 'Gemini,' and he bursts forth in praise of the brilliant stars appearing in this 'Cielo Stellato,' or Heaven of the fixed stars.

It is in consequence of this allusion to the constellation of Gemini that the date of Dante's birth has been fixed between May the 18th and June 17th—the sun then being in that constellation when he 'first felt the Tuscan air.' (*Par.* xxii, 117.)

The amazing realism of the descriptions in this poem makes it hard at times to believe them to be but the result of vivid imagination, and not really visions seen by Dante's mortal eye. In this is shown his great genius, the power he possesses of carrying one away with him and making his descriptions life-like and convincing. 'Not by art does the Poet sing but by power Divine,' says Plato.

Place yourself in thought beside Dante after he describes how he has been swept up the golden ladder. Standing by Beatrice he looks down from the vantage-ground of the Heaven of Fixed Stars, and surveys each of the seven spheres which he imagines to have been visited on his upward flight.

Exhorted by Beatrice to have his eyes unclouded and acute, now he had drawn so near to 'ultimate salvation' and was ready to be presented to the triumphant throng who were coming rejoicing through the ether, he turned back and looked down upon the path along which he had come. He described how he saw the earth and smiled at its ignoble appearance, he saw the daughter of Latona (the Moon) shining with no shadow upon her brilliant surface. He sustained now the sight of Hyperion (the Sun) and recognised Mercury and Venus circling close to it. The temperate planet (Jupiter) between the fiery son and frigid father (Mars and Saturn). All the seven were displayed, showing them swift and distant while Dante was 'rolling with the eternal Twins' . . . 'then to the beauteous eyes mine eyes again I turned.'

Canto xxiii opens with graceful lines in which a mother bird perched on a bough beside her nest, watching for the first sign of dawn in order to find food for her young ones, is used as a symbol to describe the appearance of Beatrice, when she stood erect with clear eyes looking into the depths of space from which came onward the glistening hosts of the triumph of Christ, headed by the King of Saints, shining with effulgence of light.

> As when in nights serene of the full moon
> Smiles Trivia among the nymphs eternal
> Who paint the firmament through all its gulfs,

Saw I, above the myriads of lamps,
  A Sun that one and all of them enkindled,
  E'en as our own doth the supernal sights,
And through the living light transparent shone
  The lucent substance so intensely clear
  Into my sight, that I sustained it not.
O Beatrice, thou gentle guide and dear!
  To me she said: 'What overmasters thee
  A virtue is from which naught shields itself.
There are the wisdom and the omnipotence
  That oped the thoroughfares 'twixt heaven and earth,
  For which there erst had been so long a yearning.'

Par. xxiii, 25 : LONGFELLOW, transl.

Suddenly Dante describes his mind as opening
out to receive the teaching of Beatrice, and
though trembling with the weight of his pon-
derous theme he betook himself 'unto the battle
of the feeble brows' and strove to gaze upon the
'fair garden which under the rays of Christ is
blossoming.'

Quivi è la Rosa in che il Verbo Divino
  Carne si fece; quivi son li gigli
  Al cui odor si prese il buon cammino.

Par. xxiii, 73.

There is the Rose in which the Word Divine
  Became incarnate; there the lilies are
  By whose perfume the good way was discovered.

LONGFELLOW, transl.

The Saints like lilies appeared before him as in a flower-decked meadow stretched out under the Sun's rays :

> As in the sunshine, that unsullied streams
>> Through fractured cloud, ere now a meadow of flowers
>> Mine eyes with shadow covered o'er have seen,
> So troops of splendours manifold I saw
>> Illumined from above with burning rays,
>> Beholding not the source of the effulgence.
>
> *Ibid.* 79 : LONGFELLOW, transl.

In this Canto of rare beauty the poet describes 'the troops of splendour illumined from above with burning rays,' and the beauteous Flower, the Blessed Virgin, whom he invoked day and night, encircled by the Angel Gabriel who descending swept around her like a coronal. He hears the alluring music of the celestial lyre wherewith was crowned the Flower which gives the clearest heaven its sapphire blue, accompanying the hymn 'I am Angelic Love'; and describes the *Primum Mobile* so nearly reached and stretching far into space, as 'The royal mantle of all the volumes of that world, which most fervid is and living with the breath of God and with His works and ways.'

The King of Saints.
Ancient Italian woodcut.

[To face p. 218.

The Saints remained in sight singing the
'*Regina Coeli*,' whilst Beatrice addresses them
and begs them to give Dante a foretaste of the
heavenly feast.

> O Sodalizio eletto alla gran cena
>   Del benedetto Agnello, il qual vi ciba
>   Sì, che la vostra voglia è sempre piena ;
> Se per grazia di Dio questi preliba
>   Di quel che cade della vostra mensa,
>   Anzi che morte tempo gli prescriba,
> Ponete mente all' affezione immensa,
>   E roratelo alquanto !   Voi bevete
>   Sempre del fonte onde vien quel ch' ei pensa.
>
> *Par.* xxiv, 1.

> O Company elect to the great supper
>   Of the Lamb benedight, who feedeth you
>   So that for ever full is your desire,
> If by the grace of God this man foretaste
>   Something of that which falleth from your table,
>   Or ever death prescribe to him the time,
> Direct your mind to his immense desire,
>   And him somewhat bedew ; ye drinking are
>   For ever at the fount whence comes his thought.
>
> LONGFELLOW, transl.

The answer was given with so divine a song
by the fiery spirit of S. Peter whirling around,
that the poet is nonplussed by the magnitude of
the fantasy and hesitates to describe it.

Però salta la penna, e non lo scrivo ;
Chè l'imaginar nostro a cotai pieghe,
Non che il parlare, è troppo color vivo.

Par. xxiv, 25.

Therefore my pen jumps up, and I write it not ;
For our imagination can no more bend to it
Than our speech, it is too vivid a colour.

Canto xxiv and the two following ones describe the examination of Dante when brought face to face with the three great Apostles, S. Peter, S. James and S. John, who, in answer to the urgent appeal that some little foretaste of the Heavenly feast should be vouchsafed, respectively question him upon the three theological virtues, Faith, Hope and Charity. Girding himself 'like a man taking his Bachelor Degree,' Dante falls back firmly upon the Holy Scriptures and gives his devout reply as to Faith in the words of Hebrews xi, 1, ' Faith is the substance of things hoped for, the evidence of things not seen.' Being further pressed he explains the definition of the words and produces replies which obtain for him a chorus of joyous melody in a *Te Deo Laudamus*, and a three-fold blessing from S. Peter. Thus encouraged he then looks forward to the supreme moment when he may perchance return to his Font of Baptism in Florence, showing the never dying Hope which dwelt in his mind, making it easy to hold himself bravely when questioned as to the 'greatest of gifts;' by S. James, although alas! that special longing was never granted.

Prompted by Beatrice, 'the pitiful one who guided the feathers of his wings to so high a flight,' the answer is given :

> 'Speme' diss' io, 'è uno attender certo
> Della gloria futura, il qual produce
> Grazia divina e precedente merto.'
>
> *Par.* xxv, 67.

To quote Peter Lombard: 'Hope is the certain expectation of future bliss, coming from the Grace of God and from preceding merit.' Not only the hope of a future life and the redemption of the soul and spirit, but also the redemption of the body from sin and evil during this mortal life, that 'earnest expectation of the creature,' alluded to in Romans viii, 18, 'waiting to be delivered' and to enter into the glorious liberty of the children of God.

Verily Dante understood the true meaning of Hope and joyfully listened to the words '*Sperino in Te*,' which rang above and echoed all around at his answer.

Perhaps unduly elated with the success of his examination, Dante presses forward to gaze too intently upon the burning light of the Apostle of Love—S. John; the result being that on turning to ask advice of Beatrice he is appalled to find that 'though near to her and in a blissful world' he cannot see her. He has been bereft of sight through the amazing brilliance of the third light!' This passage no doubt is intended to convey the idea that the height, breadth, and depth of the love of God is quite beyond Man's vision, and can never be fathomed by human understanding. Reassured somewhat by a voice proceeding from a spot where S. John's light was placed, intimating that his blindness would pass, he shows in the following beautiful lines how successfully he has cultivated the virtue of patience and can at last humbly wait for guidance.

Io dissi: ' Al suo piacere e tosto e tardo
  Vegna rimedio agli occhi che fur porte,
  Quand'ella entrò col fuoco ond' io sempr' ardo.'

Par. xxvi, 13.

I said : ' As pleaseth her, or soon or late
  Let the cure come to eyes that portals were
  When she with fire I ever burn with entered.'

Then Beatrice demonstrates how everything tends to show that all good proceeds from God, of which the death of Christ for man is the great example, this had drawn him, ' out of the sea of twisted love,' and placed him on the right side of the river and made him love the Saints who ' like leaves make green the garden of the eternal Gardener.'

The whole Heaven resounded with the song of ' Holy, Holy, Holy,' and thus awakened, Beatrice clears from his eyes the mist and enables him to see better than before.

With sight restored and made keener, Dante tells how the first father of mankind, Adam, discerns his wish for information and relates the reason of the Fall, namely, ' not tasting of the tree, but disobedience to the Divine will' (line 115).

Adam alludes to the Holy Name of *J.* or *Jah* by which he called the Almighty before he left this earth (line 133) and in the last lines of this Canto refers to the short space of his sojourn in Paradise.

There is a tradition that Adam remained *alone* in the Garden of Eden for 500 years, but only six hours after Eve came with her unrestrained desire for knowledge. If Landino's reading be followed which has a comma omitted after 'dishonesta,' the last four lines of Canto xxvi read thus :

> Nel monte, che si leva più da l'onda,
>   Fu io con vita pura, e dishonesta
>   Da la prim' hora a quella ch'è seconda,
> Come 'l sol muta quadra, a l'hora sesta.

The translation might then read : 'On the mount, which most doth rise from out the sea, was I pure, and disgraced from the first hour to that which follows the sixth hour, as the sun changes quadrant' (*i.e.* up to the beginning of the seventh hour), thus leaving his previous stay a matter of conjecture, his whole life having been 930 years.

The *Gloria* begins again, and a very 'smile of the Universe' seems to pervade the Cielo Stellato, when suddenly S. Peter bursts out with flaming ardour against him 'who usurps my place on earth, my place, my place'—namely, Pope Boniface VIII. This is one of the famous passages often referred to, full of denunciation against the corrupt practices of the Church. The poet's attention wrapt in considering these things needs to be recalled by a reproof, as he gazes after S. Peter passing out of sight, and contemplating again the face of his sovereign lady it appears so wonderful 'that surely God Himself must have rejoiced in her countenance.' Her look raises him into the 'ciel velocissimo.'

> E questo cielo non ha altro dove
>   Che la mente divina, in che s'accende
>   L'Amor che il volge e la virtù ch' ei piove.
> Luce ed amor d'un cerchio lui comprende,
>   Si come questo gli altri; e quel precinto
>   Colui che il cinge solamente intende.
>
> *Par.* xxvii, 109.

Primum Mobile

> And in this heaven there is no other Where
>   Than in the Mind Divine, wherein is kindled
>   The love that turns it, and the power it rains.

P

Within a circle light and love embrace it,
  Even as this doth the others, and that precinct
He who encircles it alone controls.
                                    LONGFELLOW, transl.

Plato is here followed, as may be seen in the *Timaeus* where he says : ' The soul framed by the will of the great Creator is interfused everywhere from the centre to circumference of heaven. . . . The Creator finished His good work by causing to be woven together mortal and immortal elements to form living creatures. . . . To these He distributed souls equal in number to the stars, assigning to each soul a star ; and He showed to each the nature of the Universe and His own decrees of destiny ; declaring that whoever lived a religious life upon earth should return again to the habitation of his star and then have a blessed existence. . . . The Creator being free from jealousy desired that all things should be as like Himself as possible.'

From the *Dialogues* of Plato, transl. Jowett.

THE ANGELIC HIERARCHY

Gazing into the 'beauteous eyes of her who did imparadise his mind' Dante is aware of a most brilliant reflection therein, and looking back he finds the centre of this heaven to be filled with effulgence of light. It comes from the abode of the Almighty Creator and Mover of the Universe, from whence, surrounded by nine revolving circles of glorified beings, love and knowledge are poured forth. Not until the mists are again cleared from his eyes can the poet venture on a description. Thus :

> Come rimane splendido e sereno
>   L'emisperio dell' aere, quando soffia
>   Borea da quella guancia ond' è più leno,
> Per che si purga e risolve la roffia
>   Che pria turbava, sì che il ciel ne ride
>   Con le bellezze d'ogni sua parroffia ;
> Così fec'io, poi che mi provvide
>   La donna mia del suo risponder chiaro,
>   E, come stella in cielo, il ver si vide.
>
> *Par.* xxviii, 79.

'Even as the hemisphere of the air remains splendid and serene when Boreas blows from that cheek whence he is mildest, because purged and resolved from the rack which first disturbed it, the heaven laughs with its beauties on every side ; thus did I, when my lady provided me with her clear answer, and like a star in heaven, the truth was seen.'

Then is explained to him that the two circles nearest the centre are formed by :

1 {
  1 The Seraphim, who love most, and
  2 The Cherubim, who know most, and these together with
  3 The Thrones—form the first Triad.

2 {
  1 Dominations,
  2 Virtues,
  3 Powers, form the second Triad.

3 {
  1 Principalities,
  2 Archangels,
  3 Angels, form the third Triad.

The three-fold melody of 'Osanna' resounds perpetually throughout the angelic ranks.

Their occupation is thus imagined by Hettinger :

'The first Hierarchy contemplates the power of the Father; the second the Wisdom of the Son ; and the third the Love of the Holy Ghost, Whose gifts it transmits to us.   Each person of

the Trinity can however be apprehended in a
triple relation, and for this reason each Hierarchy
has three orders.'

> All, as they circle in their orders, look
> Aloft; and downward, with such sway prevail,
> That all with mutual impulse tend to God.
>
> *Par.* xxviii, 117.

'In accordance with mediæval teaching the
nine choirs of Angels move the nine celestial
spheres, and by means of them control the
elements. But their special work is amongst
mankind.'

With eyes fixed upon the Light enchaining
Dante's vision, Beatrice gives a reply to questions for which, without his defining them she
knows he anxiously desires an answer. She sees
in the Light of all Truth how the great Creator
shows forth the reflected splendour of His love,
not for His own good but in order that human
beings may apprehend His existence (Canto
xxix, 15). She describes the immeasurable
company of Angels, each having their own
special ray of knowledge and love, reflected from
above as it were into many mirrors; and she

sternly deprecates the wandering off of mortals to vain doctrines and foolish inventions, since Christ gave His disciples charge to keep to 'the true foundation.' (*Par.* xxix, 109.)

THE VISION OF THE BLESSED TRINITY

Empyrean   Like stars whose light fades at the coming of dawn, the glittering circles are veiled by a brilliance of greater power, and turning to his guide for information, Beatrice tells him that the Empyrean is now reached—the Heaven of Heavens which is 'pure light,' and perfect calm. (*Par.* xxx, 39.)

Here 'intellectual light, the beholding of God with the intellect, perfect love arising consequent on the vision, and joy coming from the possession of supreme Good,' as Ed. G. Gardner says, 'receive their consummation.'

The beauty of the smile of Beatrice has become so marvellous that Dante declares the sequence of his song, begun at the moment 'when first he saw her face in this life,' must now be ended ; it baffles the description of finite man, only the

Omnipotent can truly understand the perfection of Divine Wisdom.

Wrapped in a veil of light the poet can see nothing, until the words:

> Ever the Love which guideth this heaven
> Welcomes into itself with such salute (saving grace)
> To make the candle ready for its flame,

put power into his vision enabling him to see the wondrous river.

> E vidi lume in forma di riviera
> Fulvido di fulgore, intra due rive
> Dipinte di mirabil primavera.
> Di tel fiumana uscian faville vive,
> E d'ogni parte si mettean nei fiori,
> Quasi rubin che oro circonscrive;
> Poi, come inebriate dagli odori,
> Riprofondavan sè nel miro gurge;
> E, s'una entrava, un' altra n'uscia fuori.
>
> *Par.* xxx, 61.

> And I saw light in semblance of a river
> Tawny with splendours in the midst of shores
> Painted with blossoms of a wondrous spring.
> Forth from this stream there issued living sparks;
> And on all sides they mingled with the flowers,
> Like rubies that smooth bands of gold environ.
> Then as though drunken with the fragrances,

> They plunged again into the marvellous tide;
> And as one sank another issued forth.
>
> J. Addington Symonds, transl.

Dante's thirst for information obtains an explanation from 'the Sun of his eyes,' even Beatrice, who bids him drink of the water in order that the symbolical meaning may be made clear. The draught from the river being a type of the gift of the Holy Spirit by which he received virtue to see celestial things. So, bending his eyelids down into the marvellous tide, he sees it spread out wider and wider into space till it becomes a perfect circle, and then he saw both courts of Heaven manifested.

> Oh! Splendour of God! by means of which I saw
>   The lofty triumph of the realm veracious,
>   Give me the power to say how it I saw!
> There is a light above, which visible
>   Makes the Creator unto every creature,
>   Who only in beholding Him has peace,
> And it expands itself in circular form
>   To such extent, that its circumference
>   Would be too large a girdle for the sun.
> The semblance of it is all made of rays
>   Reflected from the top of 'Primal motion,'
>   Which takes therefrom vitality and power.
>
> *Par.* xxx, 97 : Longfellow, transl.

Thus Dante cries; and in one wide circle of vision these wondrous courts of Heaven are revealed to him. Within the yellow centre of the eternal Rose which breathed forth an odour of praise Beatrice drew him saying: 'Behold how great the concourse of the white-robed multitude, see how large our city circleth'! The thrones are not all filled, and Beatrice points out one with a crown upon it, on which should sit the soul of Henry of Luxembourg, looked upon as Italy's saviour had not his life been cut off too early, soon after this was written.

It is impossible to do more than glance at the last 3 Cantos, contemplative Cantos as they are termed, every line is of rare beauty, but only by a close study will a true grasp of their meaning be gained, to the delight of the reader.

'In searching for silver, gold will be found,' as says our Poet in his Convito.

The fact is here brought home to us that perpetual brooding upon exalted subjects enriched Dante's mind with keener perceptions than that of most other mortals, or he may have been vouchsafed visions of beatified glory enabling him to give to the world this wondrous imagery. Even as great artistic painters bring forth in line and colour the emanations of their brain, so did Dante in line and verse voice his poetic and beautiful imaginations, leaving them behind him to raise mankind; bidding them dwell with the mind's eye upon glories of the unseen Heaven, even as they endeavour to pierce with mortal vision the glory of the sapphire sky.

Canto xxxi begins with the description of the multitude of the redeemed arranged like petals around the calyx of a full-blown rose, ministered to by showers of sparkling Angels bringing peace and love in their upward and downward flight.

In forma dunque di candida rosa
Mi si mostrava la milizia santa
Che nel suo sangue Cristo fece sposa ;
Ma l'altra, che volando vede e canta
La gloria di Colui che la innamora,
E la bontà che la fece cotanta,
Sì come schiera d'api, che s'infiora
Una fiata, ed una si ritorna
Là dove suo lavoro s'insapora,
Nel gran fior discendeva, che s'adorna
Di tante foglie, e quindi risaliva
Là dove il suo Amor sempre soggiorna.

Le facce tutte avean di fiamma viva,
  E l'ali d'oro, e l'altro tanto bianco,
  Che nulla neve a quel termine arriva.
Quando scendean nel fior, di banco in banco
  Porgevan della pace e dell' ardore,
  Ch'egli acquistavan ventilando il fianco.
                                    Par. xxxi, 1.

In fashion then as of a snow-white rose
  Displayed itself to me the saintly host,
  Whom Christ in His own blood had made His bride,
But the other host, that flying sees and sings
  The glory of Him who doth enamour it,
  And the goodness that created it so noble,
Even as a swarm of bees that sinks in flowers
  One moment, and the next returns again
  To where its labour is to sweetness turned,
Sank into the great flower, that is adorned
  With leaves so many, and thence reascended
  To where its love abideth evermore.
Their faces had they all of living flame,
  And wings of gold, and all the rest so white
  No snow unto that limit doth attain.
From bench to bench, into the flower descending,
  They carried something of the peace and ardour
  Which by the fanning of their flanks they won.
                                LONGFELLOW, transl.

This exquisite opening seems to carry us in
thought straight along a shaft of light, into the
glorified presence of those who have gone before

—up into Divine Peace through the intercession of the Lamb of God. The bending petals of the white rose in clearness like unto alabaster, form seats whereon the jewels of God's crown are placed in holy safety, surrounding the centre heart which is of pure golden light—the eternal emblem of majesty. But behold! only half the Rose is completely filled. In this is clearly brought before us the Communion of Saints in all its breadth of meaning. Those souls who have joined the Church Triumphant are pictured as waiting in expectant hope and peace, moving throughout the Heavenly Courts when they desire, or when sent by God on errands of love, but waiting, always waiting for the arrival of those who are militant here on earth, and looking towards and returning ever to the spot where perfect Love abides. All idea of materialism must be put aside; everything being of a diaphanous nature nothing obscures the penetrating light. The 'miro gurge,' or wondrous river, which widened into a perfect circle under Dante's astonished eyes, streams down from the height of the Empyrean in an effulgence of light

upon the *Primum mobile*, and is reflected back
again up through the centre of the Rose, in this
light the radiant saints, rank upon rank, are
mirrored.

Well may Dante pray in this realm of bliss.

> O Trina Luce, che in unica stella
>   Scintillando a lor vista sì gli appaga,
>   Guarda quaggiuso alla nostra procella !
> *Par.* xxxi, 28.

> O Trinal Light, that in a single star
>   Sparkling upon their sight so satisfies them,
>   Look down upon our tempest here below !
> LONGFELLOW, transl.

Then he ' who to the divine from the human,
from time unto eternity had come, and from
Florence to a people just and sane,' turned with
amazement to his sweet guide for information,
but instead of his beloved lady he finds an old
man at his side, who, in response to his instant
cry of ' She, where is she?' points to her seat in
the third row of the redeemed ones to which she
has returned, after effecting the rescue of the
wanderer from his difficulties.

Dante lifts his eyes, and beholding Beatrice

crowned with the eternal rays addresses her and
offers her thanks in these touching words :

> ' O Donna in cui la mia speranza vige,
> E che soffristi per la mia salute
> In inferno lasciar le tue vestige,
> Di tante cose, quante io ho vedute,
> Dal tuo podere e dalla tua bontate
> Riconosco la grazia e la virtute.
> Tu m'hai di servo tratto a libertate
> Per tutte quelle vie, per tutt 'i modi,
> Che di ciò fare avean la potestate.
> La tua magnificenza in me custodi
> Sì, che l'anima mia, che fatt'hai sana,
> Piacente a te dal corpo si disnodi !'
> Così orai; ed ella, si lontana
> Come parea, sorrise e riguardommi ;
> Poi si tornò all' eterna Fontana.

Par. xxxi, 79.

> ' O Lady, thou in whom my hope is strong,
> And who for my salvation didst endure
> In Hell to leave the imprint of thy feet,
> Of whatsoever things I have beheld,
> As coming from thy power and from thy goodness
> I recognise the virtue and the grace.
> Thou from a slave hast brought me unto freedom,
> By all those ways, by all the expedients,
> Whereby thou hadst the power of doing it.
> Preserve towards me thy magnificence,
> So that this soul of mine, which thou hast healed,
> Pleasing to thee be loosened from the body.'

Thus I implored; and she, so far away,
  Smiled, as it seemed, and looked once more at me;
  Then unto the eternal fountain turned.

                LONGFELLOW, transl.

This is intensely human and full of pathos; the smiling down upon him from her far-off seat, looking with loving eyes upon him, and then turning to the Fount of all joy, as if entreating him to follow swiftly.

S. Bernard the ancient Abbot of Clairvaux (A.D. 1153) type of contemplation, takes the place of Beatrice as guide during the short span of the vision yet remaining. He may have been chosen for this post on account of his devoutness and energy in founding Cistercian Monasteries and dedicating them to the Blessed Virgin. Directing Dante's gaze upwards, he points out the arrangement and position of those blessed ones forming the Mystic Rose.

Imagine Dante drawn like a bee into the immense centre of the wondrous flower. Raising his head in amazement his eyes wander round the distant outside edge, until they rest upon the spot where the rays of light seem most concentrated. There, seated in a delicate white petal, he beholds the Blessed Virgin Mary holding the most exalted place. Below her a line of Hebrew dames are seated. Eve the mother of all living being at her feet, then Rachel beloved of her husband, and Beatrice beside her. Sara type of fidelity, Rebecca type of prudence, Judith who showed great liberty of soul, Ruth the ancestress of Christ and others 'went down the Rose petal by petal,' but not quite so far as the centre, for a circle round the golden calyx is here imagined of 'spirits released before they had made their choice, and who by their faces and childish voices could be recognised as infants.'

A most beautiful thought, this joyous multitude of holy innocents who by the faith of their parents have been brought into a state of safety and blessedness. This passage in the *Divina Commedia* must be very comforting to many fathers and mothers, who having lost their little children grieve for their brief stay on earth.

Across this central zone and forming a line on the opposite side of the Rose, S. John the Baptist takes the first seat at the outside edge of the

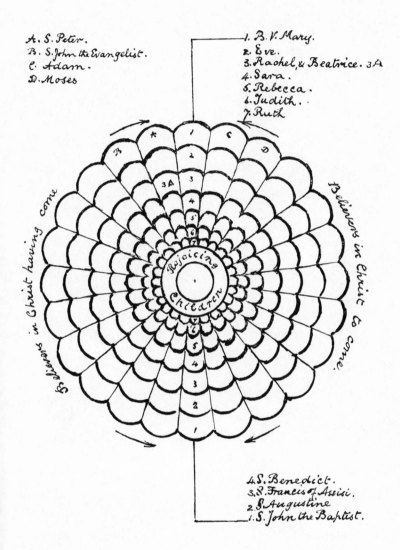

A. S. Peter.
B. S. John the Evangelist.
C. Adam.
D. Moses

1. B. V. Mary.
2. Eve.
3. Rachel, & Beatrice. 3A
4. Sara.
5. Rebecca.
6. Judith.
7. Ruth

Believers in Christ having come

Believers in Christ to come.

Rejoicing Children

4 S. Benedict.
3 S. Francis of Assisi.
2 S. Augustine
1 S. John the Baptist.

The White Rose of the Saints.

Par. XXXII

E. M. B

[To face p. 240.

petals, followed step by step as they narrow towards the centre by S. Augustine Bishop of Hippo, S. Francis of Assisi, S. Benedict and others. These two dividing lines, of Hebrew Dames and ancient Fathers of the Church, separate the spirits of those who believed in '*Christ to come*' from those who believed in '*Christ who has come.*'

Looking back to the highest point where sits the Blessed Virgin, Dante sees on her left hand Adam, Moses, and all those ancient ones who looked forward to the coming of Christ; on this side the semi-circle is entirely filled.

On the Virgin's right are placed S. Peter, S. John the Evangelist, and others who lived after Christ; the number of these being incomplete there are many vacant seats amongst the petals in this half of the Rose.

S. Bernard hastens to implore Dante to turn his eyes to the Primal Love, so that gazing towards Him he may pierce as far as possible into the shining depths of His glory. But since that is not enough to prevent a backward fall, he directs Dante to join in a glorious hymn, too long

Q

to be quoted in its entirety, imploring grace and assistance. It thus commences:

> 'Vergine Madre, figlia del tuo Figlio,
> Umile ed alta più che creatura,
> Termine fisso d'eterno consiglio,
> Tu se' colei che l'umana natura
> Nobilitasti sì, che il suo Fattore
> Non disdegnò di farsi sua fattura.'
>
> *Par.* xxxiii, 1.

> Virgin Mother, daughter of thy Son,
> Humble and more exalted than any creature,
> Predestined of the eternal council,
> Thou art she who didst so ennoble human nature
> That its Creator did not disdain
> To make Himself its creature.

Beseeching her of her tenderness to have pity upon him who from the 'deepest pool of the universe' had emerged to such a height, and yet required more power to enable his eyes to see the ultimate salvation or bliss, S. Bernard implores her to disperse all the clouds from his mortality by her prayers, and to keep sound his affections after so great a vision.

' Vinca tua guardia i movimenti umani;
  Vedi Beatrice con quanti beati
  Per li miei prieghi ti chiudon le mani!'
Gli occhi da Dio diletti e venerati,
  Fissi nell' orator, ne dimostraro
  Quanto i devoti prieghi le son grati.
Indi all' eterno lume si drizzaro,
  Nel qual non si de' creder che s'invii
  Per creatura l'occhio tanto chiaro.

Par. xxxiii, 37.

Let thy protection conquer human movements;
  See Beatrice and all blessed ones,
  My prayers to second, clasp their hands to thee!
The eyes beloved and revered of God,
  Fastened upon the speaker, showed to us
  How grateful unto her are prayers devout.
Then unto the Eternal Light they turned,
  On which it is not credible could be
  By any creature bent an eye so clear.

LONGFELLOW, transl.

Finally, the poet relates how there was accorded to him power to gaze into the depth of the great Light, and to grasp more fully the Vision glorious. In order worthily to write he prays this ' Light Supreme ' to give his tongue power to leave if only a sparkle of the glory behind for future generations to apprehend.

He tells how he beheld all and everything gathered and bound in one volume of embracing love.

> Within the deep and luminous subsistence
>   Of the High Light appeared to me three circles,
>   Of threefold colour and of one dimension,
> And by the second seemed the first reflected
>   As Iris is by Iris, and the third
>   Seemed Fire, that equally from both is breathed.
>   LONGFELLOW, transl.

Dante bursts into a cry of rapture:

> O Light Eterne, sole in Thyself that dwellest,
>   Sole knowest Thyself, and known unto Thyself
>   And knowing, lovest and smilest on Thyself.
>   *Ibid.*

and in ecstasy, he beholds the semblance of a human figure in the second rainbow-coloured circle. This new manifestation bereft him of words until in a flash as of lightning all was revealed to him, and his love and will were made one with the Divine Will.

The poem is closed with these words:

All' alta fantasia qui mancò possa;
  Ma già volgeva il mio disiro e il *velle*,
  Sì come rota ch' egualmente è mossa,
L'Amor che muove il Sole e l'altre Stelle.

To the high fantasy power here failed;
  But already my desire and will were rolled,
  Like to a wheel that evenly is moved, by
The Love that moves the Sun, and the other Stars.

END OF THE
Divina Commedia

DANTE'S RESTING PLACE

After writing these words Dante laid down his pen, his work was finished and his mighty soul went out in peace to the glorious land fortified by the rites of the Holy Catholic Church; and he who believes that the poet had grace afforded him to write this Vision for the good of mankind, to lead them to a belief in the Communion of Saints, the resurrection of the body, and the life everlasting, cannot doubt that he was met on the threshold by Beatrice, 'guida dolce e cara' and conducted to the presence of God. His mortal body was subject to strange vicissitudes. After his death, due to a fever caught when returning along the Venetian shore, the people of Ravenna gave him honourable burial, his remains resting in a chapel close to the Church of the Franciscans for about sixty-seven years. Presently fair Florence awoke to what she had done to her greatest citizen and vainly endeavoured to get

possession of them, but Ravenna would not give
them up. When some verification was sub-
sequently required the tomb was opened and
found to be empty.

Years, even centuries, passed until at length
the legend that the remains had been carefully
hidden proved true. In an interesting pamphlet
published by the Municipio of Ravenna the
strange tale may be read, and a print of the box
seen, in which the precious treasure was eventually found as late as June 1865. The actual box
with two inscriptions by Fra Antonio Santi,
dated 1677, is now in the Biblioteca Nazionale at
Ravenna. That on the outside runs:

DANTIS OSSA

A ME

FRA ANTONIO SANTI

Hic posita.   Anno 1677.

Die 18 Octobris.

The shorter one, with the words 'Dantis Ossa
Denuper revisa die 3 Junii 1677,' was also found
at the bottom of the box.

The facts of the case seem in brief to be these.

Terrified at the idea of giving up their treasure during the years between the first demand of Florence in 1396 up to 1519 when permission was at last given to the Florentines to take possession, the Franciscan monks had taken the matter into their own hands, so that when the small sarcophagus was opened it was found to be empty.

The matter was hushed up by the monks who kept the secret. Only an accident disclosed the hiding-place when work was being done to the Braccioforte chapel adjoining the Mausoleum just a month before the proposed sexcentennial commemoration of Dante's birth in June 1865. A workman struck with his spade something hollow in a piece of wall and it proved on examination to be the box containing the precious bones. They had been hidden in the Convent from 1519, and built into the wall in 1677 by Fra Antonio Santi, one of the monks well known to have lived at that date.

Frantic was the excitement of the Italian people as they came from all parts of Italy on that June day in 1865 to gaze upon the wonderful sight, and not a little pride must Ravenna have felt in having so steadfastly guarded her treasure, which she still possesses. It was proved twenty-five years afterwards, in 1890, that the monks had drawn the remains through a hole in the back of the sarcophagus, which they then filled up and thus removed all trace of their deed.

As a touch of the marvellous seems here a necessity, it is not astonishing that the old custodian, sleeping in those gloomy quarters, used to describe how he saw the shadowy figure of Dante in his red robe coming out of the wall, and passing across the dark precincts of the Braccio-forte chapel. Unfortunately the old man only lived to within a few days of the moment when his dreams would have seemed to be realised. Re-stored to their first resting place, and in a mausoleum adorned with sculpture and epitaphs, Dante's dust still reposes in the ancient city. A few years ago a lamp, the gift of Italian and English admirers, was placed over the great poet's tomb to be kept perpetually burning, but it needs no artificial light to preserve steadfast the torch of the genius of Dante Alighieri ever

pointing its flame upwards and leading mankind towards the realms of the Divine Creator.
'Who,' to use the words of S. Augustine, 'made
us for Himself, and our soul is restless until it
finds its rest in Him.'

An intense human note breathing throughout
the *Divina Commedia* attracts all kinds and diversities of readers. The literary world studies it
for perfect style, wide knowledge of mankind,
history, art, music, and philosophy, whilst for the
more spiritual seekers there shines out the
'beatific Vision,' and gleams of 'the green leaf
alive'—emblem of that perpetual hope which
makes life endlessly glorious.

As regards Dante's personal appearance and
characteristics but little is really known since
the contemporary portraits are few. The most
notable is certainly that in the fresco by Giotto
on the wall of the Bargello, but his figure may be
traced in other frescoes dating from that period,
as for example one in the lower Church of S.
Francesco at Assisi where Dante represents the
third order of the Franciscans to which he is
supposed to have belonged, and he wears the

girdle of the order round his waist. An upturned
head in a fresco of the last judgment, probably by
Orcagna, in the Strozzi Chapel in Santa Maria
Novella at Florence, depicts the great poet in
the act of adoration among the elect.

There is moreover the mask of his face which
is considered to be authentic, and it would seem
that this has had influence upon most later
pictures, inasmuch as his likeness can generally
be recognised by reason of the stern rugged lines
copied from it.

Leonardo Aretino, one of his biographers, says
'he was a noble person, peaceful and dignified
and of an agreeable countenance.'

In the critique written in August 1911 upon a
new and magnificently bound copy of the *Divina
Commedia*, Gabriele D'Annunzio calls our earnest
attention to the points of character which he finds
apparent in the outline and features of the great
Florentine.   The following is a literal translation
of the passage referred to : 'His face is placid,
chiselled with the exigencies of his own spirit,
and with the necessities of our faith.   The eye is
large, because widened by his voracious nature,

and never-ending continuous visions; deep-set and hidden in shadow because he lived to himself and in himself, like one who alone discovers the summit of the soul and pays no attention to the carnal senses. The nose is aquiline as indicating gentle lineage, imperious force and noble arrogance; and marked with a wrinkle because his thoughts cut it, and his griefs deepened it.

'Grand is the jaw and vigorous, because his lineaments were superimposed upon bones which nature had destined to grasp and grind that of which his instinct made choice.

'Protruding and pointed is the chin, because it has the iron form of a wedge which can penetrate and cleave the hardest trunk. The mouth is like a closed lock sealing up a great internal fire, enclosed by two cheeks like two defending trenches. The protrusion of the under lip above the upper is a sign of immutable disdain for injury and persistent insult.

'What may be called something sacerdotal and regal is assured by the band across the forehead, and the bands also round the cheeks, like a swathing fillet for entombment, so the figure resembles that of the risen Lazarus, even like a man raised by a miracle from the shadow of death.'

Portraits of Beatrice Portinari do not appear to exist; but the figure in the before-mentioned fresco by Orcagna, is now held by some authorities to represent the gentilissima Donna who at an early age entered into Dante's heart and remained for ever his ' Sovereign Lady.'

Allusions to a vast number of interesting passages and beautiful quotations have perforce been omitted in this slight sketch, for the immense range of the wondrous poem produces the difficulty, not so much as to what should be written but in reality what should be left unsaid, in dealing with it in a simple fashion. That this little work, the result of many years of happy study, may prove of use to busy people in bringing them more easily into touch with the *Divina Commedia*, without diving into long and learned Commentaries, is the desire of the writer, and to them it is sent forth in hope.

Speriamo di venire, quando possiamo, al glorioso porto.

TO DANTE

(*Written in Italian by* MICHAEL ANGELO)

Translated by LONGFELLOW

What should be said of him cannot be said,
By too great splendour is his name attended,
To blame is easier those who him offended,
Than reach the faintest glory round him shed.

This man descended to the doomed and dead
For our instruction ; then to God ascended ;
Heaven opened wide to him its portals splendid,
Who from his country's, closed against him—fled.

Ungrateful land. To its own prejudice
Nurse of his fortunes, and this showeth well
That the most perfect most of grief shall see.

Among a thousand proofs let one suffice,
That as his exile has no parallel
Ne'er walked the earth a greater man than he.

LIST OF BOOKS WHICH MAY BE CONSULTED

Italian Text and Commentary. Landino and Vellutello. Venice Ed. 1564.
Italian Text and Commentary. Brunone Bianchi.
Italian Text and Commentary. P. Pompeo Venturi.
Italian Text and Commentary. F. Torraca. 1908.
Italian Text. Edited by Raffaelo Fornarciari. 1911.
Tutte le Opere di Dante Alighieri. Collected by Edward Moore, D.D.
Bibliografia Dantesca. Colomb de Batines.
Dizionarietto Dantesco. G. L. Passerini.
Vocabolario Dantesco. L. G. Blanc.
Textual Criticism of the Divina Commedia. Edward Moore, D.D.
Studies in Dante, First and Second Series. Edward Moore, D.D.
Introduction to the Study of Dante. J. Addington Symonds.
Studies in the Inferno, Purgatorio, and Paradiso. G. A. Scartazzini.
Studies in the Inferno, Purgatorio, and Paradiso. W. Warren Vernon.
Essays and Addresses on Dante and Aquinas. H. P. Liddon, D.D., D.C.L.
Dante et la Philosophie Catholique au Treizième Siècle. Frédéric Ozanam.
Dante's Divina Commedia, its Scope and Value. Hettinger. Edited by
    Henry Sebastian Bowden of the Oratory.
Dante: an Essay. R. W. Church, D.C.L., Dean of S. Paul's.
The Commedia and Canzoniere of Dante Alighieri. E. H. Plumtre.
Dante and his Circle. Dante Gabriel Rossetti.
Dante's Ten Heavens. Edmund G. Gardner.
Dante and the Mystics. Edmund G. Gardner.
Dante and His Time. J. Karl Federn.
Dante Alighieri. Paget Toynbee, D.Litt.
Dante Dictionary. (Concise edition, 1913.) Paget Toynbee, D.Litt.
Dante. (People's books, 6d. edition.) A. G. Ferrers Howell.
The Chronicle of Dino Compagni. Temple Classics.
Translation. Divina Commedia (with notes). H. W. Longfellow.
Translation. Divina Commedia. H. F. Cary.
Translation. Divina Commedia. Temple Classics.
La Vita Nuova. (1911.) Michele Scherillo.
La Vita Nuova. Text and Transl. Temple Classics.